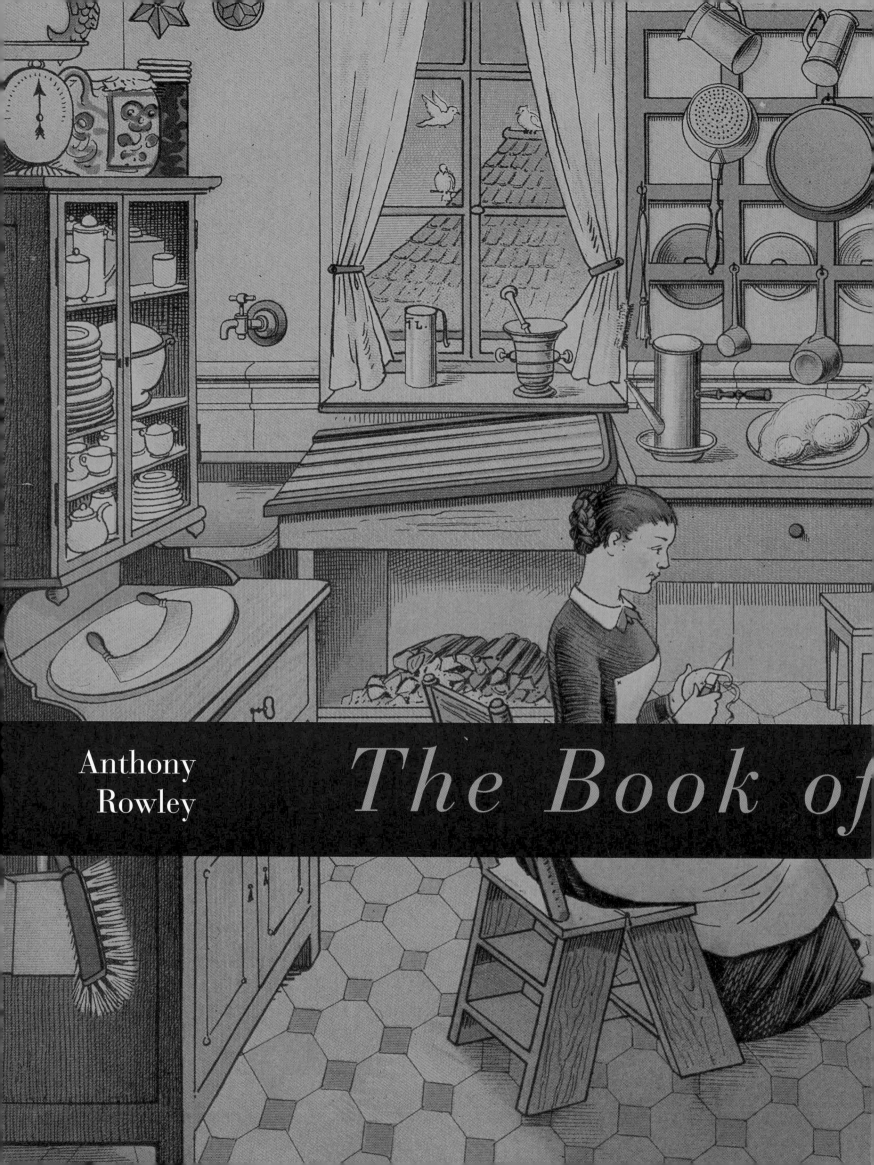

Anthony
Rowley

The Book of

Kitchens

Translated by Deke Dusinberre

Flammarion

Editorial Direction: Ghislaine Bavoillot

Design: Marc Walter – Bela Vista

Copy-editing: Bernard Wooding

Adaptation Connoisseur's Guide: Katherine Portsmouth

Typesetting by Studio X-Act, Paris

Color origination: Articolor

Originally published as Le Livre de la cuisine
© Flammarion, Paris 1999

For the English-language edition
© Flammarion, 2000

Flammarion, 26 rue Racine, 75006 Paris, France

ISBN: 2-08013-678-X

Nº d'édition: FA3678

Dépôt légal : October 2000

Printed in Italy

Contents

An Entire World in a Kitchen

"I saw a fine thing in Sainte-Menehould," reported Victor Hugo, "namely the kitchen of the Hôtel de Metz.

"Now that's a real kitchen: an immense room with copperware all along one wall, crockery occupying the other. In the middle, opposite the windows, is the fireplace, a huge cave filled with splendid fire. The ceiling is a network of beams magnificently blackened by smoke, from which hang all kinds of wonderful things: baskets, lamps, a meat safe, and, in the center, a large openwork net where vast hunks of streaky bacon sprawl. Before the fireplace, in addition to spit, chimney hooks, and cauldron, there glows and glimmers a dazzling set of a dozen shovels and tongs of every shape and size. The flaming hearth sends its flickers everywhere, creating large shadows on the ceiling, lending a pink hue to the blue crockery, making the fantastic edifice of pots glow like a wall of coals. If I were Homer or Rabelais, I would say, 'this kitchen is an entire world, with the fireplace as its sun.'

"It is a world, indeed. A world bustling with an entire republic of men, women, and animals. There are waiters, maidservants, assistant cooks, and carters seated around stoves and hot plates, plus the chortling pots, the yapping pans, the pipes, the cards, the children at play, the cats, dogs, and the chef who superintends all."

Thus the key idea was expressed, with his usual talent, by Alexandre Dumas (for it was he, in his *Dictionnaire de Cuisine*, who put these words into the mouth of his friend Victor Hugo). *The Book of Kitchens* will try, in its own way, to serve as both illustration and tribute to this idea—namely that within the commotion gripping a kitchen, there are two fixed points: the chef who oversees everything (pictured with watch and recipe in hand), and the fire around which all activity is organized, giving color and proportion to the pots, spoons, and dishes. This book will therefore recount the story of a place. Whether that place is public or private mat-

Every kitchen calls for skill and a little bit of magic. *Left*: A chef supervises a hotel kitchen in Baltimore, Maryland, in 1941. *Above*: Firelight gives a red glow to the utensils in *Still Life with Kitchen Utensils* by Dutch painter Cornelis Jacobszen Delff (1571–1643).

ters little, which is why few restaurants will figure here. As to food, we are much less interested here in the origin, quantity, and use of ingredients than we are in how they are stored, whether they are prepared in pots or stewpans, cooked on a grill or a stove. After all, even Dumas skimps on a description of food the better to describe the sounds it makes when being prepared.

The kitchen acts as laboratory and place of secret worship, subject to the dictatorship of the eye that superintends the cooking, locates the appropriate utensil on the wall or in the cupboard, determines the next move to make. Even the temptations of nose or palate—lifting a lid and tasting—are subject to the eye's authority. The kitchen is one of the rare places where gourmets, for instance, hold their peace, either because they have become cooks themselves or because they are waiting for the meal to emerge from the ovens in order to launch into their usual conversations and assessments. We should take note that Dumas, one of the most famous nineteenth-century representatives of that confraternity, respected protocol by refraining from any mention of the culinary quality of the dishes served at the Hôtel de Metz. Following his example, this book will ignore gastronomic treatises and all that special parlance triggered by the pleasure of dining, all those historical or literary anecdotes concerning a given dish.

It is hoped that readers will find themselves in a frame of mind similar to the figures depicted by Giambattista Tiepolo about 1765 in *Punchinello's Kitchen*. The haunt of the *commedia dell'arte* characters is depicted as a portion of ruined wall, a fence, and another low wall, arranged just like a stage set, thereby defining the space of culinary ritual as precisely as any solid structure. Viewers of the painting cannot know what is being cooked in the copper kettle (pasta perhaps), but the operation seems so crucial that the guests have abandoned all other activity. These characters who usually symbolize, even caricature, a hypocritical society unable to reveal its true features, a society in which what is displayed is not necessarily related to reality, here find themselves—for once—completely "unmasked."

Above: Punchinello's Kitchen (c. 1765) by Giambattista Tiepolo offers a truthful portrayal of a crucial operation: the preparation of a dish. This art has its hidden side, as revealed by Jean-Siméon Chardin's Scullery Maid (1738, *right*). But the masks of the former and the absent gaze of the latter suggest the same thing—working in the kitchen means being completely absorbed in the task.

The Magic of the Hearth

This tale opens with a theft and ends with a marriage of convenience. Formerly, fire was the prerogative of the gods. The sun, meanwhile, burned and dried more often than it cooked. Of course, people paid homage to the sun prior to heating water on hot stones—a rustic technique employed in southern France as late as the nineteenth century by shepherds to warm sheep's milk (which suggests that these stilt-wearing shepherds should perhaps be considered as the last sun worshipers). In any case, the method was so inefficient that only men, from the Amazon to Siberia, were entitled to eat sun-cooked food, as a symbol of supposed domestic superiority. Women had to remain content with raw, cold food, with whatever they gathered, with eggs they would crack on a stone before swallowing.

Kitchen cuisine only began with the harnessing of energy. In mythological tales, ruses were used to uncover the secret of the magic animal that created, maintained, and transmitted fire—whether jaguar, vulture, monkey or salamander. Sometimes, man lulled the animal's wariness by making it laugh or pity humankind's wretched fate at having to eat earth's putrescence; sometimes man captured or killed the animal, then fled with his smoking prize (which might be lost en route, going

Domesticated during the Neolithic era, "stolen from the gods" according to mythology, fire gave birth to cooking. The space dedicated to the preparation of meals was organized around it. Until the seventeenth-century development of stoves, food was cooked over a wood fire either in the open air (*above*, a sixteenth-century engraving by Théodore de Bry) or in a fireplace (*left*, apples and chicken cooking at the manor of Plessis-Josso in Brittany; *previous page*, kitchen fireplace in a Georgian home in London, occasionally opened to the public by its owner, Dennis Severs).

out for lack of fuel or extinguished by wind or rain unleashed by divine vengeance).

Such myths have both "historic" value and moral scope, recounting mankind's long quest for fire in prehistoric ages. They reveal the divide between the artistic inhabitants of Lascaux (in 17,000 B.C.) and Neolithic cooks (about 6000 B.C.). Until that latter point, the principle of survival meant stocking as much fat as possible in the body whenever food was available. But when fire arrived, first outside and later inside the cave, people were able to prepare soups made from barley and wheat; they began equipping themselves with makeshift spits, concocting grills of vines and clay, and weaving baskets that could be set directly on heated stones. If needed, the stones could function as a rudimentary pot, unless animal skins were already doing the trick. This enormous revolution was made possible by the bow and arrow, an invention as crucial to our ancestors as steam power was to the nineteenth century and electricity to the twentieth. Thanks to bows, a small number of hunters could provide regular, more abundant food; men who no longer hunted learned to domesticate animals and plant crops. Now, all of those foodstuffs had to be stored, prepared, and cooked, the very functions still performed by kitchens today. It was indeed the bow and the hunter who truly "gave birth" to the hearth—which just goes to show that myths recount the truth.

They also indicate just how hard it was to learn to domesticate fire. About 8000 B.C., people were probably still relying on chance forest fires in order to enjoy roast meat. Managing to establish a permanent hearth for cooking food meant imposing human intelligence not only over earth (people no longer had to count on chance forest fires) but also over the skies, because a hot meal meant that people could eat when they wanted, inventing special preparations and seasonings based on human techniques and tastes. Thus, about 6500 B.C., a special kind of "cooking pot" emerged: burning-hot stones were placed in the skin of bear or bison, along with meat, water, starchy roots, and some herbs. The skin was then set on a tripod of branches. This earliest version of "boiled stew" represented the rational—rather than magical—use of fire. The great Galileo

Above: A medieval English dwelling. In the Middle Ages and the Renaissance, only manors and abbeys devoted one or more rooms exclusively to cooking, separated from other living quarters. As housing became more opulent, kitchen smoke, smells, and sights were increasingly banished from the nobler quarters; sometimes the kitchen was even detached from the main building. This principle survived into the eighteenth century—at Versailles, valets had to cross a street, climb a staircase, and pass through several rooms before serving the king's meal.

was not mistaken when he pointed out, eight thousand years later, that the mastery of fire freed the human species from its bestial shackles thanks to the domestication of heat, "that most penetrating energy, capable first of making vegetal bodies fecund, then of fortifying the nature and spirit of men."

Fire elevated mankind. In return, it became the center of private space, monopolizing the vigilance of its guardians since it was the sole guarantee against a return to a state of nature. Its shape and color were observed. Silence was maintained around the fire, because it was vital to superintend the stoking and ventilation of the fire itself, the heating of slabs or

recipients (to prevent them from breaking), and ultimately the cooking of the food. This rule of silence has become a sacrosanct principle of the culinary world. Instructions remain brief and technical, because every operation is not automatically successful, and only silence is appropriate to the domestic miracle of transforming something dead and dry into life-giving nourishment. A twelfth-century French manual expressed it in almost proverbial fashion: "Taciturnity is necessary among meats." Everywhere, people are wary of loquacious chefs. In Central America there is an enduring legend around a bird called the nightjar, which has a huge beak like a toucan,

In this fourteenth-century psalter belonging to Sir Geoffrey Luttrell (1276–1345), the depiction of a kitchen shows the fireplace still located in the middle of the room. Smoke filled the air before escaping as best it could through openings in the ceiling. Also illustrated are the tasks of pounding and chopping, crucial operations in the days when culinary art was a sophisticated alchemy of strong flavors.

completely out of proportion with the rest of its body; it was allegedly punished by the gods for having laughed loudly while their august meal was being cooked. Since that time, the nightjar has had to live with its retort-shaped beak and can emit only disgusting noises, the worst possible punishment for a bird. In France, the same kind of association between cooking and noise occurs in the etymology of the word *gargote*, meaning a cheap restaurant where the food is dreadful because the pot has been boiled so long that it makes uncouth "gargling" noises. Fire brought order to the kitchen; speech and its disorder is the domain of the meal.

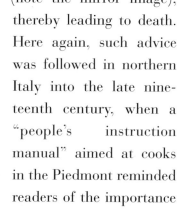

The hearth separates humankind from nature because the former has domesticated the latter: the cooking time of food is a promise of life extended thanks to human intelligence rather than the cosmic rhythm of the seasons. Fire also raises humankind above animals because humans are the sole living beings that use it to feed themselves. He who masters nourishing heat holds the secret of health and longevity, as cookbook authors never fail to point out. The Venetian chef Bartolomeo Scappi, an encyclopedist of culinary techniques and utensils who published a *Complete Treatise* in 1571, devoted an entire volume of his publication to a demonstration of the advantages for conva-

lescents of eating things as hot as possible. To this end, he published engraved plates showing kitchens in which everything was organized for maximum heat retention. One of his compatriots thought it useful to add, in 1580, that the "governance of health" involved extreme attention to heat, which must "invade the body and maintain it at a constant temperature" to avoid the risk of "extinguishing the internal fire" (note the mirror image), thereby leading to death. Here again, such advice was followed in northern Italy into the late nineteenth century, when a "people's instruction manual" aimed at cooks in the Piedmont reminded readers of the importance of domesticated heat to bodily health. The same was true in the French-speaking regions of northern Italy, where the heat of the hearth was alleged to revive the enfeebled bodies of old people, shorten the convalescent time of children and even give ideas to young women who lacked suitors. "Dancing on the back of the oven" could make people live again.

This beneficial heat nevertheless supposed that fire was constantly maintained. The question was, where? Fire is a friend as dangerous as it is valuable. Given climatic conditions and construction techniques, indoor hearth-fires appeared only in a rather narrow geographical zone running diagonally from the tip of Ire-

Previous pages: The often-copied masterpiece by Bruegel the Elder, *A Visit to the Farm* (a copy conserved in the Musée des Beaux-Arts, Le Havre), provides precious information about northern European kitchens in the sixteenth century. The farmhouse's large main room, the focus of domestic life, is dominated by an enormous cauldron in the middle. Butter is being churned in the background, behind the set table. Heat was thought to be essential to health, so everything was done to conserve it; often the hearth would be raised in order to create a pleasantly warm space on the floor. *Above*: A sixteenth-century engraving showing a raised hearth where servants can warm their feet and the cat can take refuge. *Right*: The Nuremberg house where Albrecht Dürer lived from 1509 to 1528.

land to the Adriatic. Elsewhere, fears of accident or lack of necessity led to a more or less marked disjunction between the energy and its location. In Nordic countries, therefore, fire was maintained in a kind of shed, a forerunner of the kitchen. At the other end of the European continent, around the Mediterranean, fire was almost a piece of furniture in the form of a brazier that could be carried from one room to another: no smoke, little flame, just slow heat for seafood (this type of "hearth" has found a new incarnation in the modern fashion for barbecues, also related to the new mobility of vacations and camping). This southern European item is not so very distant from the Japanese *irori*, a ceramic brazier that is the ancestor of the "chafing dish."

FIRE IN HEARTH AND HOME

Having fire enter hearth and home—it hardly matters which came first, hearth or home, so closely are these words related (the French term *foyer* even means both)—meant first keeping it going, regularly feeding it, and finally installing it somewhere. The kitchen, as a room, was born once people decided that they wanted to keep fire. Maintaining it became crucial, since the fire had to be fed before people could be fed on what it cooked. Wood was the main component of this percolating system until the late nineteenth century. If necessary, people did not hesitate to centralize their source of heat in order to insure the baking of the all-important bread, as was

The fireplace is the warm, nourishing heart of a kitchen. *Left*: *A Wealthy Kitchen* by Pieter Aersten (1508–1575, Statens Museum for Kunst, Copenhagen). *Above*: *Kitchen*, school of Campi (sixteenth century, Pinacoteca di Brera, Milan).

done in Champagne in the fourteenth and fifteenth centuries.

Fire still had to be installed somewhere: the easiest thing was to set it in the middle of the dwelling, either placed in a hollow or, more frequently, raised on a pedestal of earth or stone, thereby producing an open flame with no draft. By placing the hearth in the middle of the room, the risks of burning the house down were minimized, family cohesion was reinforced, and cooking could take place on a stone or tripod. One need merely look at the sixteenth-century painting of *A Visit to the Farm* by Pieter Bruegel (pages 16–17), a subject copied by his sons Pieter the Younger and Jan: the enormous cauldron in the middle of the painting is twice as large as the children warming themselves, like some bubbling pot of life conveying the daily ritual and generational transmission of nourishment, as discreetly stressed by the allegory of the mother breast-feeding her child.

However, the painters' brilliant images deceive us somewhat—these scenes would have been darkened by an all-encompassing smoke that was probably highly unpleasant for guests. Furthermore, as feudal society took shape, it assigned a specific status to every individual and began allocating rooms according to the task to be performed, which supposed (at least in castles) a multiplication of hearths. Thus, by the end of the Carolingian period in the tenth century, the hearth began moving toward the walls. The evolution was slow, taking nearly four centuries, as randomly observed in several noteworthy constructions, without any specific region coming to the fore. About 900, there are references to stone fireplaces being set into the walls in places such as Broick, Germany, and Doué-La-Fontaine in France. They were simple in construction, the stones being plastered with clay, but it is unclear whether the chimney was added later or was part of the original design of the castle. In general, hearths migrated toward the wall in two stages: initially a hood was set on columns above the central hearth, and only when people realized that the results were not very good did fireplaces move to the wall. This system was adopted in Cistercian abbeys and many fortified farms throughout Burgundy.

In the late twelfth and early thirteenth centuries, the transformation accelerated, notably thanks to the great population upheaval caused by the land-clearing which took place across Europe. The rise in the number of mouths to feed required improved organization in dwellings; people took advantage of the partial rebuilding of a house to replace clay-covered wooden flues with stone chimneys incorporated into the wall. The starting signal was given in the lands of the dukes of Burgundy and their German neighbors. The trend then spread from these richer regions toward other centers of power, such as the Capet monarchy in Paris, which began imitating its Burgundian and Flemish cousins within fifty years. The trend also spread through the net-

In castles and manors, the fireplace moved: wall hearths appeared in wealthy homes by the tenth century, becoming more common over the next four centuries. *Right*: *The Supper at Emmaus* (Flemish school, sixteenth century, Musée des Beaux-Arts, Lille). *Following pages*: In paintings of the period, the fire in the hearth symbolized one of the four primordial elements, all of which were present in the kitchen, as seen in Sebastien Stoskopff's *Four Elements* (or *Winter*, c. 1633, Musée de l'Œuvre Notre-Dame, Strasbourg). The variety of food on the table provides clues to cuisine in those days when everything in the universe was related—in addition to fire, there was air (the various fowl), earth (the vegetables), and water (the fish).

work of abbeys, which were not only wealthy but were also obliged to lodge and nourish significant numbers of people (pilgrims, visiting nobles, monks, and, during times of war and famine, the local peasants). The chef in a monastery was held in such high esteem that the Benedictine rule accorded him "relief" from religious obligations, given the burden of his tasks. Similarly, in the monastery at Eynsham, near Oxford, the cook is described in the consuetudinary (one of those texts that monks would compose to assert their rights against civilians and to vaunt their own merits at the same time) as being "humble of heart, benign of soul, overflowing with mercy, careful toward himself, generous toward others, a consolation to sad folk, a refuge for the sick; sober and reserved, he shall be a shield to the poor and, after the cellar master, the father of the community in everything that pertains to his functions."

Monastery kitchens were built as annexes, primarily to avoid setting the abbey on fire (buildings of stone represented progress in that respect), but also to limit the temptations for monks who might smell the odors coming from the fireplace. As a general rule, the floor plan was circular or octagonal, which was supposed to favor the evacuation of stale air and provide rational organization of cooking spaces. In French monasteries at Marmoutier and Fontevrault, the main fireplace was still central, with a conical hood to help the fire to draw; along the sides were braziers; and there were no windows (the ever-present obsession with heat), just a staggered series of holes in the walls. The cooks worked by the light of the hearth or with the help of torches. This medieval floor plan prevailed until the seventeenth century in monasteries like those at Bourgueil, Vendôme, and Pontlevoy. The only notable change was that the central hearth gave way to wall chimneys. Secular kitchens followed monastic example in intent—the kitchen began to lose the dimensions of a room were everything took place, was later moved to one end of the castle or stately home, and then became individualized around a new organization of the household, thereby gaining new annexes and growing in size once more.

By the late fourteenth century, the French example began to influence northern Italy through contact via market fairs, pilgrimage routes, and the new sociability of European courts. But progress was slow, and it was not until the fifteenth century that a northern Italian city like Prato began to re-equip itself. Change was even slower in England: about 1360, the Lord Mayor of London was particularly proud of the central fireplace that he had just installed in his castle at Penshurst Place, Kent. It would be another one hundred and fifty years until the Tudors switched to wall fireplaces, at Cotehele in Devon. It took another century and a half to convince the Baltic provinces, at which point a European revolution begun five hundred years earlier was finally complete.

"As to kitchen hearths [in Paris], they're good," wrote eighteenth-century chronicler Louis-Sébastien Mercier in his *Tableaux de Paris*. "Nothing is said of them, true enough, they are never mentioned; people never ask to see one, but if it did not exist, the sitting room would certainly be empty the whole year round." Kitchen hearths often boasted extraordinary spits for roasting whole animals. The complex machinery of spits (sometimes driven by a dog treading a turnspit-wheel) represented the first domestic appliances. *Right*: A fine spit in brushed steel, "cranked" by a little automaton, can be seen in the Hospice in Beaune, France. It dates from 1698.

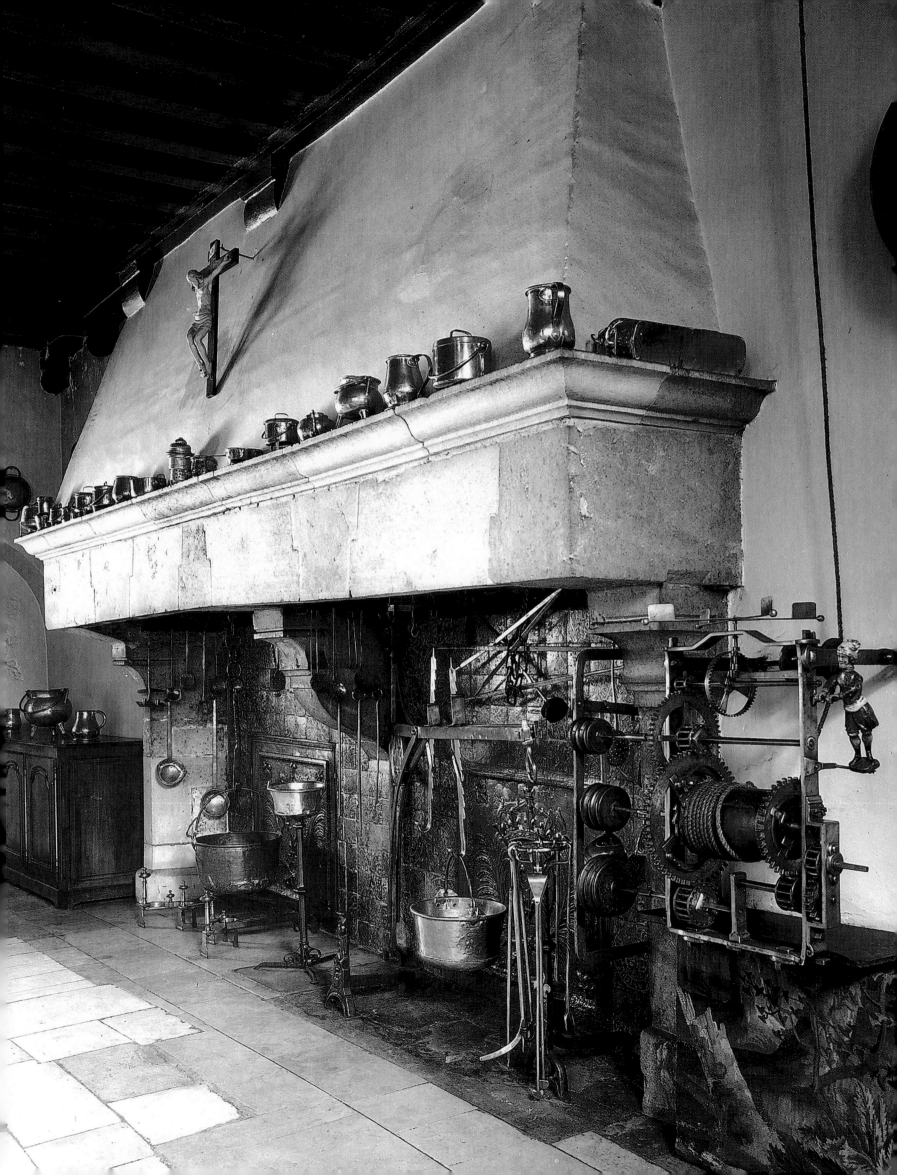

This shift altered the basic design of houses: placing the hearth against the wall forced masons to install a chimney, in general up the lateral peak of the house. Fire became a true fireplace. Its open flame provided steady heat for a soup cauldron hanging from a hook in the chimney, below which could be placed larger logs making it conceivable to install mechanical spits, even as the coals could be used to cook an egg (a dish far more frequent than meat).

Barely had the hearth found its place against the wall than it was moved again. Or rather, it multiplied, finding new places and sometimes enclosing itself. This development, in the late seventeenth and early eighteenth centuries, was prompted equally by technical advances, by a concern for culinary variety in wealthy households, and by the choice between cooking (meaning kitchen) and heating (meaning bedrooms). From the kitchen standpoint, olfactory considerations now came into play—a meal, once set on the table, should give off aromas of culinary art, whereas the odors of the products that went into preparing it (whether unpleasant or not) were consigned to a distant room. In a society that was turning civility into a cardinal virtue, this meant nothing other than stressing

the distinction between "raw" (which smelled too strong and could be borne only by cooks) and "cooked" (suited to the noses of people of taste). In addition, there was a visual dimension—everything that came out of the kitchen had to be as fine to behold as to eat, because only a "beautiful dish" could produce gustatory delight. Kitchen tasks were simultaneously valorized—without them beauty was unimaginable—and yet masked, because they should not be seen at the table. Hence the importance of fire's role in melting, reducing, and binding ingredients in order to yield their quintessence.

This social and aesthetic charter dictated that kitchens be sited underground, away from the nobler sections of the dwelling. The ones at French châteaux such as Versailles and Trianon display a rational arrangement in which each separate kitchen has a fireplace adapted to the dishes to be prepared there, the whole thing being organized in space like an ideal meal. The kitchen for first courses, for instance, had a fireplace, an oven, and twenty-eight hot plates; the roasting kitchen, on the other hand, was twice as large, with a huge fireplace holding two chimney hooks, large andirons with racks to hold the

Above: Until chimneys were developed, smoke from the fire escaped through the roof, as can be seen in this reconstruction of a first-century B.C. kitchen in an Austrian museum of antiquity. Certain regions of Europe still retain a few of these old-style hearths. *Left*: Located in the Portuguese province of Trás-os-Montes, with its harsh mountain climate, this stone farmhouse called Casa de Carvalhinha is still entirely heated by the fire in the hearth. The smoke exits through a gap in the roof tiles. More efficient were the hoods sometimes placed above the fire, forerunners of chimneys.

spits, plus an oven and sixteen hot plates. Such a setup must have created difficulties in ventilation, water supply, and drainage. Effective use of water was a precondition for mastering fire, as though the increased number of fireplaces threatened to dry everything out, which would have spelled culinary disaster.

STOVE AND OVEN

This kind of arrangement was naturally restricted to palatial residences, but it nevertheless influenced practice throughout Europe in two distinct ways.

Protestant countries in northern Europe boxed fire into an enormous structure which radiated heat through its surface, thereby launching the "stove" revolution. By 1750, a distinction was emerging between homes with the old "French hearth" and homes with stoves where the making of meals could return, so to speak, to the main room; an oven or boiler might be stacked onto the stove, yielding a "furnace." In the rest of Europe, more susceptible—or subjected—to French culinary influence, the important thing was to adapt the flame to precise culinary requirements. This explains the success, starting in the seventeenth century and extending into the eighteenth, of long brick stoves on which

The earliest kitchen stoves appeared in the seventeenth century. They were brick furnaces, often faced with fine tiles (*left*, a stove dated roughly 1820 in the château of Creil, near a famous ceramics works). Stoves introduced the principle of "contained heat" into kitchens. Wood was economized along with the heat, which was evenly distributed. Such stoves augured an era of gentle stewing and lengthy simmering. *Above*: The kitchen stove at the Hospice in Beaune, used for pharmaceutical preparations, features copper alembics.

several things could be simmered. Because they were raised, they were less tiring for cooks, who could stand straight rather than bending into the heat of the fireplace. Such stoves would be placed near a window, making it easier to evacuate the carbon dioxide produced by charcoal, notably in kitchens situated underground or in monasteries. Furthermore, small individual hot plates made it easier for the chef to monitor things, so that delicate dishes could be cooked there. Sometimes, as at Compton Castle in England, a stove was set next to the fireplace and used to cook puddings and meat pies. The attraction of the stove was the addi-

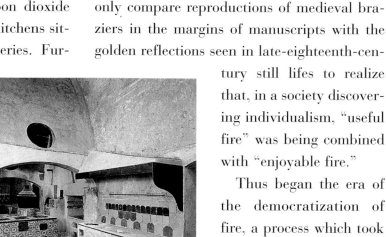

tional cooking surface it offered, away from the fireplace where other dishes were roasting and grilling. Stoves nevertheless remained an accessory until the end of the eighteenth century. They did not become a dominant kitchen item until about 1800, when they were transformed into "closed-fire ranges" made of sheet metal or cast iron. Thanks to such appliances, a cook could prepare several dishes at once (increasing efficiency) with less fatigue (reducing labor costs), since they eliminated the need for bending. These appliances would long remain the prerogative of affluent households, but modest dwellings could participate in the quest for efficiency by adopting the ancient technique of braziers. Indeed, standing a bronze chafing dish over a small amount of charcoal made it possible to prepare sauces or cook small pieces of meat or fish. One need only compare reproductions of medieval braziers in the margins of manuscripts with the golden reflections seen in late-eighteenth-century still lifes to realize that, in a society discovering individualism, "useful fire" was being combined with "enjoyable fire."

Thus began the era of the democratization of fire, a process which took place in three stages and encountered reticence on the part of servants, hesitation on the part of masters, and skepticism over a technical advance that seemed to dissipate the magic of flames, thereby diminishing the sacred mysteries of cooking. And yet the democratization was both financial (lower costs) and technical (ease of use). The Harel range, for instance, appeared about the 1820s. It was a new version of the stove, made of "brick or stone, built on a wood frame and covered with ceramic tiles, set on the hearth or before a window. It incorporated several terracotta fireplaces of various shapes and sizes, whose upper parts had a rim into which various recipients could be set." A whole meal could

The shape of the Certosa di Padula stove (*above*) inspired later stoves of cast iron, which appeared about 1830 (*right*, the château of Rasanbo in Brittany). Cast iron was an indestructible material that conducted and conserved heat excellently, and revolutionized the cook's work: the fire was contained inside, and heated an internal oven plus a broad surface at various temperatures (if often difficult to control). It thus became possible to cook several dishes at once and keep them warm along with the plates and a good part of the house (even after the fire was out). Enthusiasm for cast-iron stoves persists today, and many are still in use, whether recent or renovated like the one shown here.

be prepared with ten cents' worth of charcoal. But such ranges did not delight servants in bourgeois households, who complained of being less warm—perhaps a skillful way of complaining that the dispersion of tasks, which meant greater efficiency for the master through steadier work, also meant dissolving the community of cooks.

Twenty years later, cast-iron ranges which incorporated stoves and ovens made it possible to prepare an entire banquet: it was simultaneously possible to cook two roasts, heat two saucepans and two pots, simmer a double boiler and warm the plates. This time, servants complained about the excessive heat given off by the appliance. The cooks, mean-

while, complained of its robust efficiency: true, they could prepare a soufflé and a fish dish at the same time, but the heat never seemed to be distributed exactly as the chef desired. Chefs apparently intended to remain sole masters of precise cooking operations, and only reluctantly bowed to the technical advantages of a variety of cooking methods within a single unit. Thus the famous Jules Gouffé, chef at the court of Napoleon III, after having regaled the moneyed aristocracy at the Jockey Club for a decade, complained that a cast-iron range hampered his talents as a "decorator-chef." Gouffé was raising the old debate between art and craft, because he ultimately felt that cooking appliances should be

In France, the famous Godin company began mass-producing cast-iron stoves in 1846, thereafter making constant improvements. This 1931 model (*above*) incorporates two "hot closets" and two ovens with spring-latched oven doors. The most important advance occurred with the arrival of gas in 1850. Stoves were initially mixed, burning both wood (or charcoal) and gas, becoming fully gas-fired in the 1930s (*right,* on a farm in Canada). Thus the chore of wood and charcoal came to an end. Gas also provided a flame that was more visible, accurate, and controllable—the beginning of total mastery over heat, the almost "virtual" fire of today.

categorized according to a particular type of cuisine, cast-iron ranges being suitable for "middle-class recipes and other more basic things of domestic cuisine." Ranges also displayed a disadvantage that people thought they had already eliminated—smoke. Even when enclosed and domesticated, fire still gave off fumes, though now in the form of infernal coils rising from a subterranean world or lurking in the corners of the room. At a time when a concern for social order and hygiene was winning minds and spirits, this was a major drawback: kitchen grime was suspected of favoring epidemics, and oven smoke of aggravating the supposed laziness of servants.

Technical advances that protected cooks therefore contributed to the common good. Yet public opinion still needed convincing, because it remained both reticent and skeptical. As did professional cooks, to Gouffé's regret: "I am sorry that this new invention is still so little used, and that its great usefulness for certain cooking operations has not been sufficiently understood. Especially when steady, regular heat is wanted." In fact, gas ranges, although invented about 1850, did not become widespread in urban areas until the mid-1930s. Up till then, only little gas burners, descendants of the brazier, could be rented from the gas companies and used as cheap auxiliary cooking devices. In European countries with culinary habits still largely steeped in rural tradition, gas shortened cooking times in a way felt to be incompatible with the pace of everyday life—in the Belgian and Italian countrysides, the overly rapid and intense flame was accused of not allowing dishes to simmer long enough, nor allowing farmers enough time to milk their cows or feed the farmyard animals. More serious, though, was the impression that gas stoves sealed the victory of industrial progress, coming on the heels of central heating. Fire had thus been stripped of its traditional attributes—it was no longer granted enough time to cook and no longer performed the function of heating. The time had come for fire to bow out, to transform itself into virtual fire thanks to electricity and microwave technology.

Modern fans of gas cooking would agree with this late-nineteenth-century sales pitch: "Boiling tea ready in a minute? How wonderful! Just ask ladies who now use a gas stove if they think they could live without it!" *Left*: The stand of the ECFM gas company at the 1938 Ideal Home Show in Paris. *Above*: Three generations of a French family famous for its ovens—André, Xavier, and Adrien Dupuy. It was in 1908 that Albert Dupuy founded La Cornue, the firm which produced the first domestic hot-air gas oven. La Cornue ovens are still manufactured entirely by hand.

cooking appliances

Ancestral fireplaces first began to be replaced by stoves in the early seventeenth century, representing an initial revolution in the use of fire in kitchens. Since then, industrialization and technical progress have constantly improved cooking appliances by making them more sophisticated. Cast-iron ranges appeared about 1830, and gas models some twenty years later. Further steps in the march of progress included electric ovens in the 1920s and, more recently, microwave technology. Nowadays, manufacturers produce appliances that combine every possible cooking system, and some of them even talk of incorporating an Internet link on oven doors, in order to keep cordon bleu chefs better informed!

Gas burners All chefs claim that nothing works like a good old gas burner when it comes to heating pans and cooking up tasty dishes. Its modest price, reliability, conveniently visible flame, rapid heat, instant reaction time, and compatibility with all kinds of recipients and metals make gas an unsurpassed culinary tool. So, even if gas burners are not always ideal for lengthy simmering or ease of maintenance, they are now enjoying a marked comeback among manufacturers of ovens and stoves. They now feature several useful improvements, such as burners specially designed for Chinese woks or large fish kettles. And for people who fear the danger of the open flame (especially parents), crafty manufacturers have developed mixed stoves with induction or ceramic plates in front and gas burners in the back, away from small children.

Electric elements There was a time in France, back in the 1960s, when gas had a bad reputation and everybody began building houses that were "all electric." Deprived of gas lines—or simply convinced by major press campaigns—droves of housewives went out and bought electric stoves. In France, that meant solid cast-iron discs rather than the harder-to-clean coil elements. This led to an era of hit-or-miss cooking, of endless waiting for the disc to heat up (and then for the milk to boil over), of burned fingers and stubborn stains. Those problems resulted from the extremely long reaction time of such discs, from the fact that they always look the same regardless of their temperature, and from the nature of the material. These drawbacks still

The magic of gas has been available to all for a century now. *Far left*: An extra-large burner produced by *Gaggenau* for use with a wok. *Vignettes*: A powerful triple-flame burner, designed by *SMEG* (*top left*); the first model of the La Cornue oven, 1905 (*middle*); a 1934 Godin oven (*left*).

exist, and are not offset by the usefulness of electric elements for long-simmering dishes. These days, their only selling point is their modest cost.

Ceramic stove-tops: Elegant ceramic stove-tops offer the somewhat mysterious spectacle of a vibrant black surface glowing with noble geometric patterns, often responding to the gentle pressure of a touch-sensitive button. Made from a ceramic glass extremely resistant to heat and shock, they are a fine example of the high tech reigning in today's kitchens. Introduced in the United States in 1968, ceramic stoves are now the most common substitute for gas ranges. Electric coil or halogen elements (with infrared lamps), which react faster than traditional discs, are placed beneath the glassy surface. Here again, however, temperature control is not as precise as gas—to prevent milk from boiling over, the saucepan has to be removed quickly. In order to imitate the swift and accurate reactions of gas burners, some manufacturers offer sophisticated systems that make it possible to raise or lower the heat almost instantaneously. Unlike standard stoves, the surface surrounding the heat source remains cool, resulting in a saving of energy and reduction in burns.

On the other hand, ceramic stove-tops are not easy to care for—users have to be careful to avoid scratches, traces of calcium deposits, and corrosion caused by burned sugar. Furthermore, since the element only heats materials in direct contact with the surface, recipients must have a very flat and smooth bottom; dark, mat bottoms diffuse the heat even better. Finally, to avoid energy loss, the diameter of the recipient should match that of the burner (and, above all, be no smaller). Pans with a smooth, thick, stainless steel bottom are recommended.

Induction Another sophisticated technology is "magnetic induction" cooking, which is even safer than a ceramic stove-top insofar as the heat source is a coil underneath the glass surface that creates a magnetic field triggered

Thanks to their reliability, robustness, and functionality, the finest traditional stoves offer cordon bleu chefs advantages worthy of professional ovens. *Left*: A Rayburn stove with the cover of one of its two hot plates (it works on gas, charcoal or oil). *Below*: La Cornue's Château model incorporates two ovens, one electric and the other gas. *Bottom*: The old oven in the kitchen at Château Smith Haut-Lafitte, renovated by specialist restorer Alain Boisserenc.

With the arrival of electric, ceramic, and induction stove-tops, not to mention microwave ovens, flames have disappeared from many kitchens, leaving a virtual fire compatible with design requirements and the quest for beauty. *Left*: A Bulthaup stove-top. *Below and bottom*: Two ceramic units with digital controls (by SMEG and Miele respectively). *Right*: A built-in microwave oven by Roche-Bobois.

only when in contact with a pan on the burner. Not only does this make it safe, but also very energy efficient and simple to maintain (spills do not stick to the surrounding surface, which remains cool). Moreover—and above all—induction offers rapid control comparable to that of gas burners: the required heat is reached instantly and can be lowered instantly. The nature of induction requires that pans be of conducting metals (ferrous metals that stick to a magnet), and special stainless steel utensils have been designed for it. Because it heats the sides as well as the bottom of the pan, induction allows for savory dishes simmered, for example, in enameled cast-iron casseroles. Safe, practical, and efficient, the

only drawback to induction is its high cost. In addition to great ease of use, induction's slick, cool surfaces, futuristic lights, touch-sensitive controls, and digital displays give users the reassuring feeling of possessing a "clean," completely controllable, almost virtual heat source.

Microwaves Invented in the 1950s, microwave ovens became truly popular in the 1970s, bringing about a veritable revolution in the kitchen by considerably reducing cooking times. At first they met with some resistance: how could such high-frequency waves—which penetrate to the core of food, making water molecules stir and jostle until they generate great heat—really be safe? Wasn't there the danger of cooking your own molecules every time you walked in front of the oven? Furthermore, even though they did indeed cook, microwaves could neither simmer nor brown food. Once scientists and doctors reassured people, however, consumers enthusiastically adopted microwave ovens—not so much for cooking as for reheating prepared dishes or defrosting frozen foods. The invention made itself at home.

The microwave oven—with its revolutionary technology, luminous buttons, automatic programs, rotating platter, and bell—is probably the most obvious symbol of modernity in today's kitchens. It is now widely used and has benefited from improvements that compensate for initial drawbacks. Stores now offer ovens that combine microwave and grill functions, so that dishes can be browned. Some turntables are even designed to brown the bottoms of pizzas and quiches, and certain models incorporate a rotisserie with spit. For people not content with these strictly culinary improvements, one manufacturer has even announced a microwave-television unit linked to the Internet. Finally, widespread acceptance of microwave ovens has spurred the production of numerous specially designed utensils, implements, and furnishings.

Modern ovens Today's ovens combine a conventional source of heat ("convection") with microwaves, grill, and roasting spit, as well as "fan-circulated heat" which makes it possible to roast meat on all sides without turning it over. Still others combine traditional cooking and steam cooking in two separate sections, while some manufacturers equip their ovens with doors that remain cool during cooking, and most offer ovens that clean themselves via pyrolysis (elimination of grime through very high temperature), catalysis (absorption of grime by oxidation during cooking), and now also hydrolysis (with water).

Today's ovens are easy-to-use products of sophisticated technology. *Top left:* This multifunction model by SMEG includes a self-cleaning oven. *Above:* A Gaggenau oven. *Right:* A multifunction SMEG oven; *far right,* a SMEG oven with a safety rail to prevent pots from falling in a toddler-filled kitchen.

GAGGENAU

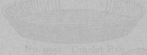

Kitchen
Utensils

All kitchens present familiar features, a familiarity that stems from common practices, childhood memories, and a feeling of permanence. A visitor's eyes will immediately seek out the hearth (yesterday's fireplace, today's cooking range), the sink, the table, the jars, and cupboards; implements can be pictured lying in the drawers. Even though the culinary day has changed more in the past half century than in preceding periods, techniques and rituals remain astonishingly long-lived. The advice offered by Taillevent in his book *Viandier*, written fully six hundred years ago, on how to "rescue" a dish that has stuck to the pan, is still perfectly valid. And contemporary hosts or hostesses would be delighted by the counsels given in "The Parisian House-Keeper," written about 1392 by an anonymous disciple of Taillevent, explaining how to use spatulas and spoons when blending sauces and preparing soups. Finally, if you compare estate inventories from the fifteenth century with the arrangement of the kitchen at Compton Castle about 1700, it becomes clear that kitchen tasks are as sacrosanct as they are straightforward—prepare,

wash, cook, and clear away. Yet it is the implements, materials, and objects employed in those tasks that truly lend life to a kitchen.

That is because these utensils are mandatory go-betweens in all culinary rites. This has been true since the dawn of time, to judge by the vestiges of archeological digs in caves dating from 20,000 B.C. Prehistoric cooks arranged their implements on long trays of stone, set at variable heights on blocks of granite. A concern for meticulous organization of the kitchen space existed in an almost natural state in certain societies in the American West and Japan. The ordering of objects, notably those used for survival, was perceived as civilization's guarantee against the threat of cosmic disorder and chaos.

It is no coincidence that an eclipse of the sun or moon was associated, by those societies, with a rebellion of objects against their masters. Should the source of heat, light, and growth suddenly disappear, then culinary implements will no longer be subject to their human masters. It is indeed technical mastery that permits the transition from coarse product to dressed ingredient, that transforms raw food into a cooked meal, that even insulates, if necessary,

The golden reflections on copper utensils and glazed pots found in traditional kitchens evoke the culinary pleasures to come, as suggested by these copper vessels from the famous Dehillerin shop in Paris (*previous page*) and in a *Kitchen Interior* (*left*) by Dutch artist Hendrik Sorgh (1611–1670). Kitchen implements are nevertheless appreciated primarily for their efficiency, as exemplified by an old chopping knife so perfect that it has never been replaced by a machine (*above*, from Bachelier Antiquités). *Following pages*: A still life painted by Jean-Siméon Chardin about 1730, *Kitchen Objects Arranged on a Shelf: Copper Pot, Mortar and Pestle, Leek, Onion, Three Eggs and Little White Jug.*

a scalding dish from the diner's mouth. Again, all these usages distinguish humans from animals—a repast must be contrived.

Relying on estate inventories and illustrated plates, then, let us view the kitchen as a family album handed down through the generations. It contains objects and arrangements theoretically inspired by technical considerations, yet which carry the unmistakable trace of a culinary lineage. In medieval kitchens, everything was organized around the fireplace, the stone sink, and a small cupboard. In the middle of the fireplace sat an iron cauldron, surrounded by smaller pots. In front of the fire were tall andirons with hooked spikes for hanging such utensils as a ladle, two-pronged fork, and skimmer. All these were used, according to Olivier de la Marche, the talented chronicler of the two most famous banquets of the fifteenth century, the chivalric Vow of the Pheasant (1453) and the wedding of Charles the Bold (1468), "for trying soups and broths, as well as for chasing children from the kitchen." On both sides of the fireplace would be set simple planks of wood to hold the pans, grills, strainers, mortars, cheese graters,

and so on. An abundance of jugs, bowls, and other recipients would be stored near the stone sink, while the salt box would be over by the cupboard. The salt box would have a wooden cover that tips up, whereas the cupboard would always be locked because it contained precious spices. In French, the kitchen cupboard was sometimes just called the *cuisine* (kitchen), probably because it gave dishes their prevailing flavor.

This description might appear to fit a manorial, high-ranking kitchen. In fact, social hierarchy was revealed more by the size of the room and, as far as utensils went, by how they were arrayed, as well as by the rooms next to the kitchen which held the tables and cupboards, the number of which was the true measure of the normal number of guests (the Louvre castle in the days of Charles V boasted nine kitchen cupboards). Nor were copper and silver utensils the sole prerogative of the royal court in Paris—a tour of kitchens in provinces such as Burgundy and Toulouse would certainly turn up silver spoons, as recommended by manuscripts of the day for making the best sauces. In general, provincial kitchens were as well equipped in techni-

Age-old tools have always been used for those sacrosanct kitchen tasks of preparing, washing, cooking, and clearing away. The kitchen is a place of order, a place where humans have to deploy skill and effort in mastering nature's most savory gifts. *Left*: Thomas Jefferson's kitchen in Monticello, like many others, almost looks like a small factory. *Above*: A more religious view of a medieval interior with fine copper pot and towel is provided by the central panel of the *Mérode Altarpiece*, painted about 1425 by Robert Campin (active 1406–44), known as the Master of Flémalle, one of the founders of the Flemish tradition.

cal utensils as Parisian ones: sieves, scissors, spatulas, cutting boards, mortars, and even—in Burgundy—special needles for pulling snails from their shells. Fireplaces, on the other hand, remained relatively rudimentary, with puny tripods, few hooks, limited pots. As to the likes of jugs and bowls, they were used for everything from preparing the meal to cooking, eating, and storing it; copper had already relegated the earthenware pot inherited from the Romans to the antique shop. Even among the poorest peasants—nearly one-third of whom had no significant possessions to will to their children—there are surprising examples of an "all-purpose" pan and a "cauldron with two wooden spoons" owned by a couple of farm servants who apparently had neither bed nor home. One key utensil was the mortar and pestle, found in every inventory (and made of every material), because it was used to grind seasonings or forcemeats (pepper for the rich, beans for the poor), not to mention almonds for dessert. People ground things constantly in order to have ingredients handy to flavor a sauce; if need be, when traveling they might take ground garlic—or even the mortar itself. Indeed, when kitchenless, people carried

at least this key utensil, the traveling companion of both beggars and princes alike.

Kitchen arrangements changed little as the fifteenth century eased into the sixteenth, yet houses themselves were evolving, as noted when comparing Dürer's *Saint Jerome in his Cell* with Robert Campin's *Annunciation*. The books, cushions, and lamps in Dürer's picture are so many domestic novelties, whereas the Flemish fireplace could be three hundred years older. Less noticeable are the candle holders, suggesting that cooks also wanted to be "enlightened" by knowledge. In fact, Renaissance kitchens reflected the extent of the technical standardization that was occurring in Europe from north to south.

Let us first take a look at the "model kitchen" proposed by Bartolomeo Scappi, chef to Pope Pius V (1566–72). His first principle was that a kitchen is initially an architect's business: "The kitchen should preferably be placed in a spot removed and protected from the public. It should be built on flat land and, above all, it must be cheerful, airy, and well arranged, with broad, high fireplaces." The second principle concerned organization: "Mantelpieces should be vast, with

Above and right: The mortar was the most crucial implement in medieval cuisine, and is mentioned in every surviving kitchen inventory. It is still employed for every type of cuisine on the planet. Used to crush or grind all kinds of ingredients, it can be made from a wide range of materials from wood and granite to porcelain, brass, and marble.

iron hooks and pegs on either side. Several iron bars should also be set into the walls to hold the chains."

Returning to the four main operations mentioned above—preparing, washing, cooking, and clearing away—it is not hard to comprehend Scappi's specific organization of space. In order to dress meat, a large knife is set on the first worktable, while at the other end of the room is a mortar and pestle. Scappi is careful to mention the presence of objects that he feels to be indispensable, although he does not bother to mention what material the mortar is made of, so here he is probably referring to a series of mortars: spices would be ground in a metal one (which does not absorb their flavor); sugar would be crushed with a marble pestle in the form of a club (later used to mash Jerusalem artichokes that arrived from the Americas); ordinary ingredients would be pounded in a wooden one. A rolling pin was used to make pastry. Two cooking areas were divided into five specific zones depending on technique employed, from grilling to basting. There were only two main kinds of cooking instrument: skewers and round recipients of the cauldron type. A wicker hive held the upright knives and spoons that the cook would reach for when cutting or serving onto the plates arranged on a third table (which confirms the impression that Scappi's model kitchen is primarily designed for a palace). Once the meal was served, utensils could be cleaned under two faucets linked to a cistern.

Unused meat would be hung from the ceiling or stored in wall chests (forerunners of meat safes), which were beginning to appear in kitchens at this time.

Rational organization of kitchen space was less evident in commoners' homes and public inns. There, cooks tended to follow local practice, which meant they were left unmoved by encyclopedic tastes. For example, in southern France mortars reigned over knives (which were more common in the north), probably due to an abundant use of herbs and vegetables, a hypothesis reinforced by the presence of sieves, strainers, and graters which were used for preparing not only the household bread but also pasta, first noted early in the reign of Francis I (about 1510–20), in kitchens in Bologna and Aix-en-Provence. Most noteworthy, in fact, are two things that "disappeared": water and tables. The sink was now often transferred to a scullery and, even more frequently, limited to a kind of stone trough in which not much would be washed. In practice, food was washed with water drawn from a well, either in a large bucket or, for speed, in a small bowl or basin. As to tables, they also moved out of the kitchen into the main room (except in inns and monasteries, where kitchen tables still served simultaneously as shelves for storing dishes, planks for chopping, and sideboards for clearing).

Renaissance cuisine vacillated between a chef's dream (à la Scappi) and "modern convenience." There were no revolutionary improvements, just a confirmation of the primacy of

Left: In every kitchen some things are displayed (on shelves and racks), others hidden (in small cupboards and drawers). Yet the proper place for things is often a question of time—the charm of certain kitchens derives from the harmony of furniture and utensils which have a shared history. Such is the case with this kitchen in the château of Menou, central France, built in a former service room. Its owner, interior designer Jacques Garcia, wanted to re-create the atmosphere of his grandmother's kitchen, to recover his own childhood.

stewed and boiled dishes. Alongside the caul-dron, that "king of the kitchen" which slowly relegated other pots to the back shelf, arrived a cooking vessel called an *oulle*. It entered France from Spain via Italy (the Spanish possessions in Naples); depending on size, an *oulle* could hold three, five or eight porringers (a small bowl for porridge or broth, often used as a unit of measure in recipe books), thereby becoming a common measure for the average cook. This small cauldron—it is worth noting the steady reduction in size of dishes in the latter half of the Middle Ages—could also be used for making soup, hung from one of the hooks on the trammel or set on a trivet. Inspired by the latter arrangement, such bulge pots soon sprouted their own legs, lifting them above the immediate flames. The pot emigrated from kitchen to table just as iron (followed by copper) was unseating earthenware vessels. Transformed into a soup pot, the *oulle* was then endowed with a lid, always of iron, and pieces of special thick cloth whose use was explicitly mentioned in estate inventories, namely to grasp a scalding pot and to remove and replace the lid. Hence the political message behind Henry IV's

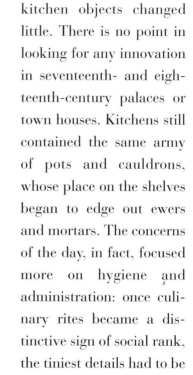

Chaudronier · Chaudronier

indefatigable defense of "sharing the pot" during France's wars of religion: his contemporaries understood that a hot chicken stew symbolized the reconciliation of families around a dish suited to every pocketbook, to be enjoyed by diners who were once again peaceful farmers instead of soldiers.

For a long while, the range and use of kitchen objects changed little. There is no point in looking for any innovation in seventeenth- and eigh-teenth-century palaces or town houses. Kitchens still contained the same army of pots and cauldrons, whose place on the shelves began to edge out ewers and mortars. The concerns of the day, in fact, focused more on hygiene and administration: once culinary rites became a distinctive sign of social rank, the tiniest details had to be respected. As a result, from Versailles to Naples and from Trianon to Stockholm, bills for "purveyances" rose to dizzying heights. One Paris burgher bought braces of aprons every two years, acquired kitchen towels by the dozen every autumn, and received the crockery and pot dealer twice a year. In 1791, after three generations of a household that never numbered more than ten—servants included—the

Copper began replacing earthenware vessels during the Renaissance (*above*, an itinerant copper merchant in an eigh-teenth-century German engraving). The warmest and most handsome of kitchen materials, copper is also preferred by many cordon bleu cooks for many dishes. It might never have fallen from favor if it had been easier to care for. *Right*: The copper *batterie de cuisine* in the kitchen of the château of Champ de Bataille, built about 1660. The kitchen was used until the early nineteenth century and, along with the rest of the interior, was carefully restored to its eighteenth-century appearance by Jacques Garcia. *Following pages*: The shop of Bachelier antique dealers, specialists in old kitchen items. Collectors the world over flock to their stall at the Paris flea market.

inventory included six cauldrons, one large boiler, eight copper bulge pots (*oulles*), nine tin-plated pots, five earthenware pots ("two of which, broken"), and all the rest that went with it, down to the stepladder required for shelves that henceforth rose to the ceiling to accommodate this *batterie de cuisine*.

It is tempting to think that Parisians were an exception. Yet estate inventories that survive for Roman and Florentine homes, as well as for the burghers living in the Spanish provinces to the north (present-day Belgium and the Netherlands) leave no doubt. In 1775, for instance, a cloth merchant bequeathed the following items: thirty-five saucepans with handles, four bulge pots, two oval pots, and ten stew-

pans—all in copper. Three years after the merchant's death, his son ordered eight more saucepans and a stewpan, even as he took delivery from Paris of two round saucepans and a "turbot kettle, in as much as I have a fine sauce cook."

It should nevertheless be noted that the boom in copper items—which give paintings of the time the impression of an additional light source, not unlike the chiaroscuro candles with which La Tour and Caravaggio lit their kitchen scenes a century earlier—was related to a new concern for hygiene. As the *Dictionnaire œconomique* pointed out, "Kitchens should be ordered as cleanly as possible." In both châteaux and town houses, that meant finding a way of bringing in clean water and draining waste water, because the private wells dug inside the house or shared with neighbors in the courtyard were drying up or becoming polluted. Nor did water carriers have a better reputation. There remained public fountains, but they were too few in number. Since water was a rare item, it had to be stored—so people used pots made of copper. The health consequences of that decision can be imagined. Thus the château of Versailles adopted the principle of "sand-lined fountains," which mean that water was run through a filter of sand before being used in the kitchen; the use of tin increased considerably and earthenware pots even made a marked comeback. Finally, by the early eighteenth century, pots and pans were systematically lined with tin.

In fact, from the sixteenth to the eighteenth century, the kitchen evolved more in appear-

Beginning in the late sixteenth century, cleanliness in the kitchen became a major household concern. It naturally required a convenient supply of water, the key agent in cleaning. It might flow from a faucet pumped from a fountain (*above*, seventeenth-century house in Amsterdam with fountain pump, Delft tiles, and stone sink) or be stored in an earthen pot or copper cistern (*right*, Chardin's *Cistern*, c. 1733).

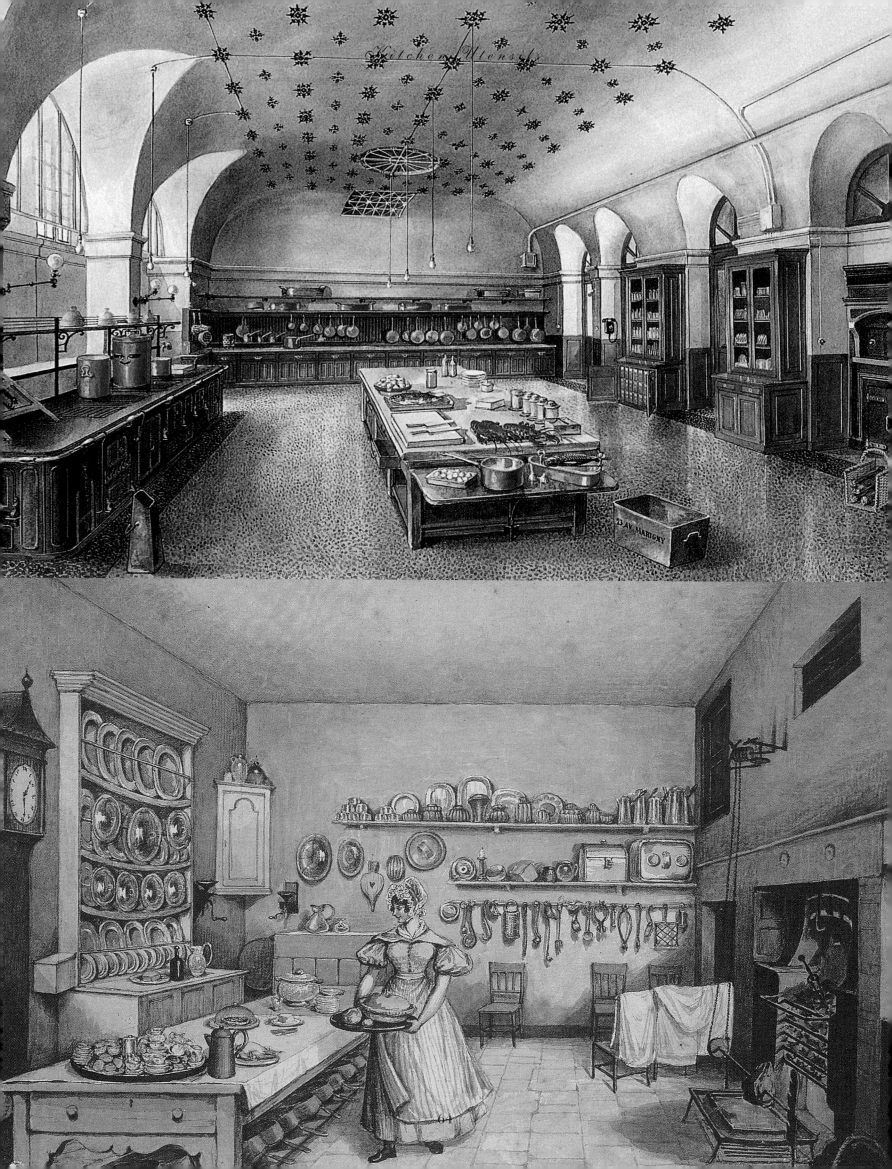

ance than in techniques. There was a social reason for this development, namely that kitchens had become the most pleasant spot in the house at a time when the pleasure of being at home had come back into fashion. Hosts in those days would show off their kitchens and utensils to guests; if need be, the most gleaming items would be painted on the wall. And although etiquette at Versailles did not allow guests to be taken into the kitchen, everyone knew, as chronicler Louis Sébastien Mercier wrote in his descriptive *Tableau de Paris* in 1790, that "visitors were drawn to a salon hearth only by a lofty kitchen hearth" because it is the latter "that makes a man famous and commendable." The social reason for the change in kitchen appearance was accompa-

nied by two technical reasons. The first was the accurate mastery of time, symbolized by the clock carefully depicted in descriptive images of English kitchens as showing 1:30 P.M., or dinner time (today's lunchtime), justifying a display of numerous patés and pastries. The second was the progress made in the copper, tin, pewter, brass, and finally cast-iron industries, which gave true meaning to the expression *batterie de cuisine* (pots, pans, and other kitchen utensils). Thus the rows of stewpans—recipients with flat bottoms, as opposed to rounded pots—can be explained by the popularity of stoves and, sometime later, ovens that called for "handy" vessels with handles. Stewpans appeared simultaneously in France and Great Britain in the mid-eighteenth cen-

The rationalization of kitchen space began in the eighteenth century and continued into the twentieth, responding to a desire for greater efficiency and cleanliness (*top left*, the light and airy kitchen of the Paris residence of Baron Gustave de Rothschild, dating from the second half of the nineteenth century) or the need to make better use of limited space (*above*, a kitchen car on the royal train in India, 1905). Furthermore, cuisine was being revolutionized through greater control over timing, which made it possible to refine the way food was cooked and to transmit precise recipes. Many depictions of large English kitchens include a clock whose hands often show 1:30 P.M., the time when "dinner" (today's lunch) was eaten, as seen in this drawing (*lower left*) by Mary Ellen Best (1809–1891) of her grandmother's kitchen at Langton Hall.

tury, first sold individually and then, about 1770–75, in sets of assorted sizes. As a general rule, people bought a set of three, but the kitchen at Langton Hall, painted about 1830, boasted ten or more. Meanwhile, "jelly" and dessert molds occupied part of a high shelf along the wall; contrary to popular belief, the "jelly" was not necessarily sweet or fruity like jam. Jelly molds, made of metals like copper or of earthenware, took the shape of a castle, as distinct from dessert molds, which took the shape of animals or flowers. A pudding mold can also be glimpsed in one corner.

This profusion of dishes and plates had to be stored somewhere. Up until the eighteenth century, modest folk did not concern themselves too much about that—they simply stacked "the dishes" on waist-high shelves. The more wealthy, meanwhile, would hang their utensils on pegs, later adopting the shelves used by the poor but raising them to the ceiling. Still later, they began shutting their pots and pans in chests and their plates in cupboards, all set into the thick stone wall in imitation of the cupboard alcoves advocated by Scappi in the sixteenth century. Early kitchen "dressers" combined culinary and practical design: a small sideboard at waist level was already being used to prepare ingredients, above which rose storage shelves while underneath were kept all the plates, pots, and pans. These three elements merely needed to be joined together to "create" the first dresser, the pride of every household regardless of social rank since it rose up to the ceiling.

Shelves and racks did not disappear, however. Cooks found the latter providential, and the same could be said—in the medical sense of the term—of the long-handled skimmers and spoons hanging there, since they enabled cooks to protect themselves from mortal burns in the fireplace (it is worth noting that domestic accidents remained France's second leading cause of "ordinary" female mortality after childbirth up till the early nineteenth century).

Storage and safety remain major priorities for modern kitchens. There is no longer any question of an "ostentatious" display, however, no floor-to-ceiling indication that a family has risen above a state of everyday hardship. Toward the end of the twentieth century, utensils and recipients were hidden to emphasize a linear geometry based on the vertical thrust of cupboards, which intersected the horizontal path of work surfaces, encircling the kitchen like battlements. Visitors may still spot *one* saucepan in gleaming copper, a rack chosen

Ever since they appeared in the Middle Ages, racks have been a feature of kitchens. All objects with handles, such as graters, whisks, sieves, and salad spinners, can be hung from them. A rack displays implements, unlike a drawer or cupboard which hides (and protects) them, so it was formerly designed not just to hang but also to exhibit one's riches. However, once kitchens became slick places where everything had to be put away in cupboards, racks were reserved for only the most decorative objects, usually of gleaming copper or stainless steel. These days, openness and visibility in the kitchen are valued, and consequently racks are reappearing.

mainly for its shape, or a shiny stainless-steel grater or strainer suggesting that implements should be as "decorative" as they are efficient. The spotless look is accompanied by a clear concern for safety—being rid of a lethal fireplace is no longer reassuring enough in an age when everyday cooking operations can be triggered by a finger. This explains the appeal of Pyrex, which combines safety and practicality (no need to transfer scalding food from one recipient to another) with attractiveness (handsome enough for the dining table), as well as the widespread use of Teflon, the anti-stick surface invented in 1950.

And yet the twentieth century would not be very noteworthy if its improvements stopped there. After all, cooks have always been concerned to shield themselves from the flames of the household furnace and to exploit every tiny space. As to graters, choppers, tureens, and the like, it is hard to see how the twentieth century contributed much that was new.

In the twentieth century, people were mostly preoccupied with saving time—a time that was devoted less to the ritual superintending of nourishment than to the monitoring of its biological, health, dietary, and medical qualities—and they wanted to be able to eat "anytime" in

the same way they wanted four-wheel-drive cars that could go "anywhere." Given such universal accessibility, the choice of utensils becomes less important than their playful potential: the backs of drawers teem with slumbering molds in the form of comic book characters, cartoon figures, and even astrological signs.

Fortunately for the twentieth century, three strokes of genius won it entry into the halls of fame: objects were revolutionized by the appearance of plastic; operations were transfigured by the development of the vegetable mill (which paved the way for blenders); and culinary ritual was transformed by the arrival of pressure cookers. The pressure cooker initially received a cool welcome, however, since this modern pot's casing was too heavy to appear attractive. Furthermore, the need to seal the top lent a certain "obscurity" to the cooking process, which henceforth occurred invisibly, literally out of the cook's visual control. Pressure cookers displayed further contempt for a chef's experience through the addition of a train whistle and a timing system worthy of the railways. Thus public rumor had it that the machine was declared dangerous when first marketed in 1927; moreover, the name "pressure cooker" suggested turn-of-

"You can certainly use one to make most dishes adequately . . . and even wonderfully if you avoid, for example, using these hermetically sealed wonder-cookers for everything and anything just because they 'save time.' They steam, discolor, soften, and cook, of course, but they're not cooks!" These comments in Vincenot's *Cuisine de Bourgogne* were expressed by many people as soon as "pressure cookers" appeared in the late 1920s (above). They perhaps explain why the pressure cooker did not meet with approval in France until after World War II, when it was renamed the "Cocotte-Minute."

the-century anarchist bombings more than gastronomic delights. It made no difference that the various French models—Lilor, Record, Viteco, and Perfecta—invoked the name of Denis Papin, who invented a steam cooker called a "soup digester" back in 1680: a stewpan was a handsome thing, whereas a pressure cooker had only its prowess to offset its ugliness. Nor did the Great Depression of the 1930s do much to change things. It was only during wartime, when food was scarce and energy short, that northern Europe discovered the virtues of fast pressure cooking: the various ordinary brands were even joined by a Hermès pressure cooker. So had it triumphed? Not quite, because in 1954 the Paris Ideal Home Show rejected SEB's Super Pressure Cooker, sparking a crisis in kitchenware whose dramatic overtones almost matched the scandal of the Salon des Refusés that launched the Impressionist movement. There was even a leaflet which would have been right at home in that artistic quarrel:

> I'm a poor pressure cooker,
> rejected by the Show.
> Yet I'm Safe and Reliable
> and Pretty, as you know. . . .
> I befriend our government
> by bringing costs down.
> I'm your friend, heaven-sent,
> 'cause I know my way around.

Signed, "Miss Pressure Cooker '54"!

Sometimes, utensils display wit. The ones employed to mash vegetables tested their wits long before potatoes came along, but to little avail: lumps always remained. So when Jean Mantelet brought a vegetable press to France from Leipzig in 1932, it met with equal lack of interest even when transformed into a mill. In the twentieth century there was no point in a utensil deploying all its wits unless it offered consumers that rarest of everyday things: a saving in time, at a reasonable price. Vegetable mills did ultimately allow cooks to leave the kitchen faster (or to concentrate on elaborat-

Left and above: Another time-saving device was the vegetable mill, a forerunner of electric appliances. Jean Mantelet invented it in 1932 (based on a German fruit juicer), but the founder of the Moulinex company only became rich and famous when he took the idea one step further. "It occurred to me that some day women would get tired of turning the handle, so I immediately decided to motorize my appliance."

ing a dish), so when the inventor lowered the price by twenty-five percent they finally found their way into kitchens. Changes in habits sometimes hinge on those tiny details that embody the headiness of freedom and change.

People in Burgundy say that "the calendar has been flipped back" to explain that generations overlap rather than follow one another. The same is true of kitchens: a look at the list of equipment recommended by the eighteenth-century *L'art de bien traiter* (Art of Fine Catering), with its pans of all sizes and materials, reveals that today's department stores and specialty restaurant suppliers are not offering anything new. On the other hand, the hierarchy of sensory values has changed—touch and smell are now outranked by sight, as witnessed by the teeming colors and widespread use of glassware. Similarly, Terence Conran's list of the ideal *batterie de cuisine* contains only four items not included in *L'art de bien traiter*—can opener, vegetable peeler, food processor, and potato masher.

There is one major difference, though: nowadays, a "user's manual"—in the form of written recipes—has replaced the old oral transmission of skills and choice of implements. Yet this cultural loss may be accompanied by the reappropriation of utensils for traditional ends: certain farmers have used the drum of an old washing machine to devise an original electric butter churn. Convenience and time-saving motives have thereby led to the reappearance of one of rural France's most emotionally charged symbols: "home-made" butter on the kids' bread and jam. This malleability of historical periods constitutes the distinctive mark of today's kitchens. The old-fashioned coffee mill glimpsed on the wall at Langton Hall (p. 64), which everyone wearied themselves cranking, was either consigned to the cellar or is displayed as a knickknack—a sign of bygone days—after having been replaced by a slick, white electric grinder, then later by the "ready-ground" coffee sold in supermarkets. Food processors, in turn, have lost the race against time and cleanliness: what is the point of using one to obtain an overly liquid gruel if you have to devote valuable minutes to cleaning it instead of profiting from the nobility and swiftness of the operation, however imperfect?

Some kitchens of old retain distinct charm. They still communicate the habits, objects, scents, and sounds that seemed to vanish forever with our grandparents: the sound of water beating on a tin colander (*previous pages*, in the little Grietje Tump house, now a museum, near Amsterdam), a precarious stack of pots and pans (*above*, a small kitchen in southern France), and the magic of wood worked in unusual shapes, as seen in the fine racks and shelving (*right*) of the "Feitora Inglesa," the trading post built in Porto in 1790 by English wine merchants.

materials

The kitchen, as the realm of utilitarian objects and furnishings, has always been the site in the home for testing new materials that are more practical, sturdier or more efficient. From simple wood to the most sophisticated metal alloys, the materials used for kitchen utensils incarnate a brief history of technology down through the ages.

Wood A widespread yet noble, handsome, and sturdy material that projects warmth and sensuality, wood has always been present in kitchens. The only everyday object to have totally vanished is the porringer, a small wooden bowl used by rural folk for centuries. Old-style wooden mortars and pestles still survive, however. They are usually made of beech, a very solid, dense, and hardwearing wood that has long been used for large items such as rolling pins, pestles, chopping blocks, and cutting boards. Smaller utensils, meanwhile, such as spoons, salt and pepper shakers, pastry wheels, handles for knives and corkscrews, are often in boxwood, another very tough species (extensively found in the Jura region of France). The most finely worked kitchen items in boxwood were certainly the stamps with which farmwives marked their butter and bread: the stamp's geometric or floral design would be pressed into soft butter on its way to the market or into bread dough on its way to the public oven.

The revival of everything natural and authentic has favored a renewed presence of wood in kitchens, often as a replacement for plastic. Wood drying racks, for example, have returned in force after ceasing to be a common household item following the Industrial Revolution. Even the traditional hand-cranked coffee grinder has made a noted comeback. In addition to furnishings such as tables, chopping blocks, cupboards, and shelves, and classic implements such as rolling pins, cutting boards, and spatulas (for nonstick pans), kitchens now flaunt more original objects such as wooden honey spoons and bottle racks.

The materials from which objects are made give life to a kitchen: the sensuality of wood, the smoothness of earthenware, the brilliance of steel. *Far left*: Kitchen utensils in a Yorkshire cottage. *Above*: The front of one of Paris's finest kitchen supply stores, Dehillerin. *Left*: Chef Paul Bocuse holds the self-basting cast-iron pot that bears his name.

Earthenware The earliest kitchen utensils were earthenware vessels for cooking and storing, invented at the same time as other forms of Neolithic pottery. Whereas amphorae and other ancient jars and dishes often feature in museums, nowadays the fine pieces that were plentiful in the kitchens of our not-so-distant ancestors—plain terracotta, glazed earthenware or stoneware—can be found at antique dealers. They sell a whole range of everyday objects essential to domestic life, including terrines (often handsomely decorated with multicolored designs or cast in the shape of edible animals), casserole dishes, curd strainers, small vinegar casks, plate racks (to be hung on the wall), and dripping pans (for the fireplace), plus numerous dishes, jars, pitchers, bowls, spice boxes, and sundry containers.

Because earthenware was relatively heavy and fragile, it could not hold out against the spread of metal and plastic. These days, only the finest cordon bleu cooks realize that a good heavy earthenware stewpan or casserole dish with glazed lining (first rubbed with garlic to prevent it from cracking in the heat) is unbeatable for long, slow cooking of meat or vegetables over a low heat. This little secret is still known to Moroccan cooks, who refuse to replace their glazed pottery tajines with new materials. Yet the almost magic properties of earthenware are now being used for less conventional objects, such as the terracotta "chicken roasters" in which you place a chicken or other fowl, accompanied by herbs and spices, then pop into the oven—the bird will come out succulent, well browned, and flavorful.

Glass Although known and manufactured for the past five or six millennia, glass did not really arrive on kitchen tables until the eighteenth century, when English glassmakers developed thick, sturdy glass to serve as the first true wine bottles. In the following century, industrial manufacturers flooded everyday life with glasses, jars, and bottles. Glass was appreciated not only for its transparency but also because it

Above: Despite its fragility, glass has unique culinary qualities. It is transparent, does not impart flavors, and can be used in microwave ovens. *Right*: Earthenware, equally fragile and also heavy, has nevertheless enchanted gourmets since prehistoric days! It not only withstands temperatures up to 1200°C, it also suits long, slow simmering and delicious braised dishes.

Left: Tinned iron and tinplate were long the most common materials for utensils. Their simplicity contrasted with the pomp of a magnificent copper *batterie de cuisine* which an owner would proudly display (*below*, the collection at the château of Mongeoffroy in the 1960s). Although copper is ideal for cooking, it can be toxic unless lined with tin—but tinsmiths are a vanishing breed.

never absorbed the taste of food it contained. The material's ability to conserve food inspired Nicolas Appert to invent a new way of preserving foodstuffs by first boiling them and then hermetically sealing them in a glass recipient. From that point onward, jars and bottles of preserves piled up in our grandmothers' kitchens, and jams would be produced from garden fruit. A variety of other glass objects were commonly found in kitchens, such as hourglasses, lemon-squeezers, household churns, and yogurt jars.

The 1930s marked a turning point in the use of glass with the advent of unbreakable glass, invented in France under the name of "Duralex." It quickly became the standard kitchen glass. At the same time, fireproof glass dubbed "Pyrex" was becoming widespread, having been invented in America in 1915. Because thick Pyrex dishes could not only withstand oven temperatures but also looked fine on the table, they were soon being produced in every shape and size. In 1964 there appeared new pots and pans in "Pyroflam"—these white fireproof vessels were born of space research and were even tougher and more resistant to extreme changes in temperature.

In the 1970s, glass enjoyed renewed favor with the arrival of microwave ovens that could not accept metal recipients. Transparent stockpots and casserole dishes henceforth became standard kitchen items. The next decade displayed enthusiasm for everything light, natural, and transparent, spurring the creation of numerous table services in glass, including cups, bowls, and pitchers with very pure lines. This trend is still going strong today.

Iron In homes of yore, many iron vessels and implements were an integral part of hearth-side cuisine—that tough, common metal was notably used for chimney hooks and trammels, skewers and spits, fire tongs, dripping pans, frying pans, and grills. Magnificent pieces of finely wrought iron, meanwhile, are today the delight of collectors (or anyone who wants to decorate a fireplace): trivets, grills, pot-stands, chestnut pans, and so on. Equally decorative are racks for hanging utensils and the peg-rails of finely chased wrought iron formerly found in the larders of lavish kitchens (where they were used to hang meat for drying and smoking).

Before being supplanted by steel and aluminum, iron was long the most common material for kitchen utensils, whether tinned (plunged into a bath of tin) or tinplated (by electrolysis). It was used for spoons and forks, kettles and funnels, graters and choppers, sieves and skimmers, as well as iron-wire whisks and salad shakers. The first vegetable mills, like the famous Moulinex marketed by Jean Mantelet in 1956, were also tinplate.

These days, tinned iron and tinplate are no longer used except in the manufacture of pastry molds.

Copper It is hard to imagine anything warmer and more attractive in a kitchen than a gleaming set of copper pots and pans. Copper is not just attractive, however—its ability to conduct and conserve heat makes it an ideal material for cooking. Heat spreads perfectly to all parts of the recipient during cooking and responds immediately to the changes in temperature often required by sophisticated preparations. All great chefs know this, and could not simmer a sauce without a copper saucepan nor brown a simple omelet without a high-rimmed frying pan.

Unfortunately, copper is not the most practical of materials. For a start, it is heavy. Furthermore, it oxidizes on contact with air, becoming toxic. This handicap has long been overcome by tinning, that is to say by lining the inside of copper recipients with a layer of tin.

Copper's ability to conduct and conserve heat is the reason top chefs continue to prefer it. *Below*: Paul Bocuse making a sauce. *Bottom*: The kitchen of the Prunier Goumard restaurant in Paris. *Right*: Enameled cast iron is more practical, and is perfect for simmering dishes. There is even a special tray for cooking snails!

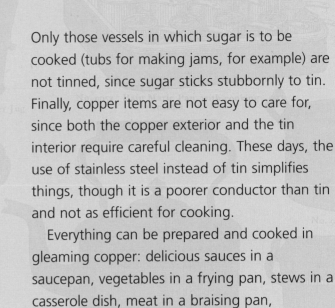

Only those vessels in which sugar is to be cooked (tubs for making jams, for example) are not tinned, since sugar sticks stubbornly to tin. Finally, copper items are not easy to care for, since both the copper exterior and the tin interior require careful cleaning. These days, the use of stainless steel instead of tin simplifies things, though it is a poorer conductor than tin and not as efficient for cooking.

Everything can be prepared and cooked in gleaming copper: delicious sauces in a saucepan, vegetables in a frying pan, stews in a casserole dish, meat in a braising pan, charlottes and whipped egg whites in a mixing bowl, soups reheated in a double boiler. Copper, unlike most other metals, can also take any form. Shiny and often finely worked items are wonderfully decorative and now tempt countless collectors. Older pieces dating back to the eighteenth and nineteenth centuries are particularly sought by collectors and can fetch hundred of dollars.

Cast iron Cast iron has been around since the Middle Ages, endowing kitchen utensils with great sturdiness and heat conducting properties. Cast-iron cauldrons and kettles, pots and pans therefore long reigned in fireplaces.

In addition to its heaviness, however, raw cast iron suffers from several drawbacks: it needs to be "seasoned" before use, which means a preliminary oiling followed by several re-oilings after initial washings (which must be done only with water, since soaps and detergent tend to penetrate the metal and leave a bad taste in food). In China, where cast iron has been used since the fourth century B.C, the large round iron pans know as "woks" must also be seasoned by oiling, and are traditionally cleaned with split bamboo sticks.

The appearance of enameled cast iron— notably the famous pot introduced by Le Creuset in 1925—put an end to these drawbacks. Maintenance is easy, heat spreads evenly, and the risks of "sticking" are practically nonexistent. Enameled casserole dishes soon

became the unrivaled queens of long-simmered dishes. The enamel may be either colored or transparent (like a varnish that allows the metal beneath to show), and can go handily from oven to table. Its eminent qualities also meant that cast iron was an excellent material for nineteenth-century ovens and stoves, which conserved heat for a long time after the fire went out. Cast-iron ovens were decorated with handsome friezes, molded foliage or checkerboard patterns of hand-painted enamel. Cast iron is still used by the makers of the most glamorous "old-fashioned" ranges, but it remains very heavy; such ovens weigh at least half a ton and require strong floors.

Steel Once sharpened, steel is a particularly good cutting material, and began replacing iron for knives at an early date. In addition to knives, other utensils designed to cut (choppers, cleavers, peelers, graters) were also

made of steel. After World War II, once it was rendered non-corroding thanks to an alloy of chrome and nickel, "stainless" steel became the king of kitchen materials. It is extremely simple to maintain, very long-lasting, resists acids, and is compatible with all kinds of heat sources. Although not perfect for knives (it is so hard that it is more difficult to sharpen than "natural" or "carbon" steel), its qualities soon won out and by the 1950s it was sweeping aside not only the iron and tin used for everyday utensils, but also the aluminum used to make pots and pans.

Sheet steel, dull and dark in color, conducts heat better than stainless steel and is highly recommended for searing and browning food at high temperatures. Deep pans and fryers in sheet steel are used above all by professionals, being generally too heavy for housewives and somewhat difficult to care for (they must be seasoned and washed without detergent).

Enameled metal Enameled sheet metal's numerous advantages made it highly common in the nineteenth century. It was sturdy, easy to care for, conducted well, did not oxidize, and imparted no flavor to food. Yet its true popularity was perhaps due to the fact that it allowed manufacturers to add color and all kinds of decorative patterns. Whereas milk jugs and kettles often came in a rich, plain color, coffeepots and sundry containers (for spices, flour, tea, coffee, and sugar) would be adorned with geometric patterns, pretty flowers, and multicolored flecks. All such decorated pieces are now highly sought collector's items.

Nowadays, the fashion for warm, more convivial kitchens has helped to revive interest in a material that comes in every color. Utensils and steamers in enameled metal have become very popular for the inexpensive touch of gaiety they bring to a kitchen.

Aluminum About 1915, aluminum began appearing in kitchens. Housewives were soon seduced by its advantages—it is as sturdy as cast iron or steel, but is much lighter and heats more rapidly. Furthermore, unlike copper and iron, it was inexpensive and easy to care for, especially when chrome plating made it "stainless" (nonoxidizing). Many kitchen utensils were designed in aluminum—deep and shallow frying pans, stewpans, egg trays, sieves, milk boxes, fruit juicers, coffeepots, and so on. Its lightness also made it an ideal material for larger items such as couscous steamers and fish kettles. Aluminum reached its zenith in the 1950s with the popularity of pressure cookers (in France alone, SEB's Cocotte-Minute has sold in the tens of millions). Another lasting invention reached the general public and changed people's lives in the early 1960s: aluminum foil. Sold in rolls, each sheet could be torn to the desired size and used above all to wrap food prior to transporting, storing or cooking it.

Aluminum cooking vessels are not very popular today, since they age poorly, tend to flake (which can give white sauces a grayish tinge), and sometimes impart a slight metallic taste to food. Above all, they are suspected of being harmful to health, although there has been no scientific proof of this to date. However, for long, slow cooking, it is preferable to use aluminum utensils that have been lined with a nonstick material.

Plastic Plastics were developed before World War II and appeared in American kitchens in the 1940s, though not on the old continent until the 1950s. It was in 1955, for example, that French manufacturers first marketed plastic basins, buckets, and garbage cans. Light, sturdy, easy to wash, and above all inexpensive, the new material could be molded into every shape and color, and therefore took the form of every kitchen item imaginable, with the exception of cutting and cooking implements. Malleability is another property of plastic, making it possible to develop hermetic storage

Below: Saucepans on the stove at the Troisgros restaurant in Roanne, France, where electricity is used for cooking. The chefs appreciate the quality of stainless steel for work surfaces and hoods. *Right*: Stainless steel reigns in today's kitchens, thanks to its easy care and handsome appearance. However, because steel is rendered "stainless" by the addition of chrome and nickel, it is not always suitable for the new induction stove-tops.

boxes that are highly appreciated for their lightness, sturdiness, and reliability, notably as marketed by the American firm Tupperware.

The kitchen has been invaded by numerous plastics such as polystyrene, polyethylene, and polyvinyl chloride. Whether colorful, satiny, fluorescent or translucent, they make fine rolling storage units as well as items like funnels, strainers, and fruit juicers.

Nonstick materials It was in 1938 that an American engineer working for Du Pont discovered polytetrafluorethylene (PTFE), a nonstick substance. It only found a culinary use in 1955, when French engineer Marc Grégoire developed a process for bonding PTFE to aluminum. In 1956, Grégoire produced his first "Téfal" pans, known elsewhere as "Teflon." Many other Teflon-coated utensils followed. Part of Teflon's popularity was due to the fact that it made it possible to cook without oil or fat, since food would not stick to the pan. This popularity was nevertheless compromised by certain drawbacks—in addition to the fact that a good sauce is almost impossible to prepare on it, the surface is easily scratched by a knife or fork, obliging cooks to employ a spatula of wood, rubber or nylon. Nowadays, a new nonstick substance is appearing on a new generation of cooking implements—an alloy of aluminum, copper, iron, and chrome which is applied in a "quasi-crystalline" film that is resistant to both heat and abrasion.

Kitchen
Space

The kitchen was long identified as the room with the hearth where meals were prepared and eaten, where people lingered in the pleasant warmth, where friends and family were received. That was still the case in a sixteenth-century manor in Normandy owned by the Lord of Gouberville. This Norman nobleman, who lived near Cherbourg, kept a diary of daily life in the years 1549 to 1563, thereby leaving the fullest surviving testimony of the life of a "gentleman farmer" during France's wars of religion. The Renaissance was nevertheless already having a marked impact on the architectural dimensions of kitchens. What normally distinguished the status of the lord of the manor was the size of his fireplace, its location, and the utensils hanging there, yet transformations were under way. They had begun in the twelfth and thirteenth centuries, and continued over extended periods often lasting hundreds of years. First there were changes to the main room, then to the organization of specialized rooms: storerooms were designed for earthenware pottery, others for food and still others—"strong rooms"—for rare objects of tin and copper. These rooms did

not necessarily open into the kitchen, but they began to come together in an embryonic suite of "kitchen offices," each with its specific function (pantry, larder, dairy, etc.). There cooks could find everything needed for daily meals—buckets, cauldrons, ladles—and for festive occasions—spits and even tables (stored in a special room because furniture for that express use was still rare). This suite already implied an extension of space, but something more was required to concretize it, to actually transform domestic architecture: if the kitchen became the main room in the house, that was because it satisfied the social ambitions of its owner, whether farmer or city-dweller, peasant or nobleman.

This evolution in architecture was not limited solely to castles or monasteries. Thus in Germany in the thirteenth and fourteenth centuries, the main room grew in length by over three feet in the homes of owners who disposed of regular incomes, whether merchants or live-stock farmers. These rooms, measuring between 300 and 350 square feet, bear the trace of a stone partition, probably designed to partly enclose the actual cooking space. Perhaps it held shelves for stacking pots, given the

Above: In the sixteenth century, the Venetian chef Bartolomeo Scappi devoted part of his life to the production of an imposing encyclopedia of culinary techniques and implements, published in 1571 as *Opera*. Its abundant illustrations offer valuable and exhaustive testimony on Renaissance kitchens. Kitchens have often served as inspiration for religious art (*page 86*, *Christ in the House of Martha and Mary* by Flemish painter Hendrick van Steenwyck [1580–1649]): the kitchen is a place for work, where the riches of nature are transformed, where labor is not confused with the sin of gluttony. *Previous pages*: *Kitchen Interior with Two Maids Preparing Food* by Dutch artist Gillis de Winter (c. 1650–1720).

frequent absence of any furniture. Subsequently the organization of space became more complicated: people sought to gain room in the stonework by creating projecting ledges, common in Ireland and Germany, or by enclosing the cooking space with an additional low wall (in England and along the Rhine), thereby marking a rectangular area that probably contained the main supplies of food and everything necessary for preparing a meal. In affluent households, two annexes then appeared, namely the bread oven and a side room for kneading the dough. Bread, as Erasmus pointed out in the sixteenth century, "holds the leading rank among those things that provide nourishment to men." In this instance, the oven reinforced the kitchen's social distinction by adding a "house" to the house. This concern was noted above all in Burgundy and the Rhineland, where prosperity—often measured in head of livestock—spurred the architectural development of farmhouses with three bays. One hosted some twenty animals, the other served as a barn, and the third was reserved for humans. This latter grew with the addition of special annexes in the fourteenth and fifteenth centuries, particularly in Saxony.

At the very end of the Middle Ages, the kitchen won greater independence when multi-storied homes began to appear. Whether due to technical considerations (rocky soil) or demographic pressure (urban density), the two-story arrangement became a sign of social status.

The dimensions of the main room were amputated by the staircase leading to the upper floor hallway, and the space shrank to the extent that guests had the impression of dining with their "rears on the coals." Ultimately, the kitchen was shoved into a corner and became separated from the main room, each one being endowed with a fireplace—one for cooking, the other for heating. This new trend—occasionally affecting inns, more frequently noble dwellings—began in Italy and slowly followed the path of profitable trade northward, pausing first in Provence and Burgundy (late fourteenth century), then in Germany (early fifteenth century), and finally England (last third of the sixteenth century). It was long thought that the practical difficulty of raising the roof explained the slowness of this spread, but in fact the know-how existed: French historian Emmanuel Le Roy Ladurie has shown that a thirteenth-century shoemaker in the village of Montaillou built an upper floor and detached his kitchen in order to flaunt his success.

In the late fifteenth and early sixteenth centuries, the kitchen became worthy of artists' attention. Its social image was more valorizing than the market scenes depicted by Bruegel in the previous century, since its religious connotations conformed to the morality of hard work—the kitchen was a place of work, and cooks were not the people who indulged in the sin of gluttony. Symbolically, meanwhile, the kitchen combined the secrets of an alchemist with the talent of an artisan. The agents of this change

Following pages: In the twelfth and thirteenth centuries, the kitchen gradually started to evolve. It grew in size and was divided into zones for various activities. Lavish kitchens were sometimes composed of several different rooms: one for kneading and baking bread, one for roasting, one for sauces, and so on, not to mention the scullery and storerooms. The kitchens at the château of Champ de Bataille included four rooms, but only the one with enormous hearth and fireplace was used as a kitchen into the early nineteenth century.

were, unsurprisingly, Italian. The first, Bartolomeo Sacchi (1421–1481), was charged by Pope Sixtus IV with organizing the Vatican archives so that they could be used for documentary reference. The political importance of this project can still be measured today by examining the fresco done by Melozzo da Forli for the pope's official quarters. It was a question of making everything new, beautiful, and true—boxes of forged documents were expunged just as rooms were made over and catalogues organized. Now, Platina (as Sacchi was known) applied this organization to the kitchen space of his day, hoping to be the first person to reconcile gastronomy (he borrowed his "contemporary" recipes from the best Italian cook of the period, Martin of Como) with notions of a healthy diet and a place of work. This meant transforming the kitchen into a scientific and medical "laboratory" even as it remained a secret temple in which a cook concocted dishes so delicious that a pope would want to taste them and acquire the recipe. Cooks thus began to pose among their utensils and the raw produce they were expected to transform; masters of the household would hold court at their banqueting tables or enjoy more

private meals plunged in contemplation of the food. Such scenes as those depicted on canvas by Cornelius van Ryck in the Netherlands, Juan Sánchez Cotán in Spain, Lubin Baugin in France, or the Soreau brothers in Germany are generally said to be mannered. Going further, we might say that they show kitchens as the scene of a domestic theater to which we do not have all the secrets. We are just barely able to identify the tools used in the operation (thanks to the prodigious visual repertoire of the likes of Scappi in the sixteenth century), along with the elements that made up the meal (as though the canvas listed all the ingredients of a recipe but offered no explanation of how to use them). Showing yet hiding—that was the key principle depicted by these artists: show the produce and the dish, hide the knack. Hide everything that surrounds the culinary rite, the food which comes from the outside, the waste that is thrown out, the dishes pulled out of the oven on their way to the main chamber or the site of the banquet; show a space that is simultaneously a shop open to the world and an antechamber to a private, closed universe.

Kitchens had already had their first heyday by the time they began appealing to artists'

Above: The proximity or availability of water remained the key problem for kitchens until the early twentieth century. In both town and countryside, certain kitchens had their own well. *Kitchen Interior* (Musée du Monastère de Brou, Bourg-en-Bresse, France) by J.B. Lallemand (1710–1805).

brushes. The dining room was now assuming the central role, at least in princely dwellings, where it benefited from a reinforcement of protocol. As early as 1624, under Louis XIII, French architect Louis Savot established a hierarchy for dining spaces as a function of social rank: large halls for princes, dining rooms for lords, a vestibule or large chamber for ranking commoners, and the kitchen for everyone else. Kitchens retained their technical specificity, but it was henceforth expected that their size be "proportional to the size of the whole building." It was no longer the cook's requirements that prevailed, but those of the master of the house. In just half a century, the kitchen would be steadily removed from the heart of the domestic scene (i.e., the dining room) and broken down into specialized units spread throughout various stories. In seventeenth-century Paris, there was such a web of partitioned annexes and closets that nearly one residence in four was organized over three stories, and one in five over four stories (or even six). The greater the number of the rooms, the wider the dispersal. Increasing the number of stories was a measure of social success, but was done in total disorder—a home-owner on Rue Saint-Antoine placed his kitchen on the

Above: Starting in the seventeenth century, urban development and the increase in multistoried buildings transformed the architectural design of kitchens once again. Now that the master of the house no longer ate in the kitchen, the problem became where to locate it and how to link it to the distant dining room. Hidden staircases and covered passages were two of the solutions employed. *Kitchen Interior* by Cornelis van Cuylenburgh (1820, Musée Municipal, Cambrai, France).

fifth floor and dined on the fourth, while another made his servants descend two floors for every meal. Connecting the kitchen to the dining area became a key concern of architects, who installed hidden doors giving access to the main stairway or contrived covered passages leading across the courtyard from one wing to another. The growing importance of dishcovers becomes understandable!

In French households, attention began to focus on the *office*, a kitchen office specializing in sweets, desserts, distillation, and the preparation of salads. The "officer" in charge of the *office*, who initially acted as the steward's jack-of-all-trades, evolved into a kind of butler who knew how to cook. He was asked to monitor the preparation of cold meals and to oversee desserts (which were mainly composed of "dry and liquid preserves"). The *office* had such little status compared to the kitchen that cookbooks of the day did not bother mentioning recipes considered unworthy of a chef's talent. And yet the *office* was concerned with decor, with the colorful staging of the final course, which is precisely what interested painters and underscored the visual rites of protocol. The

Contrasting images of European kitchens in the early nineteenth century: a modest family kitchen (*previous double page*), depicted as the cluttered realm of women in Martin Drölling's *Kitchen Interior* (Paris, 1815) differs sharply from the monumental, highly organized royal kitchen at St. James's Palace, with its army of assistant cooks and valets, its many hearths, its high ceiling and efficient ventilation (*above*, an engraving after James Stephanoff, 1819).

role performed by the *office* was thus years in advance of its recognition by cooks, and the room became a small-scale replica of the kitchen, housing several types of heat source. There was already a charcoal heating stove to keep preserved fruit dry; subsequently a cooking stove was added for the copper basins used to prepare caramels, jams, and—after 1690–1700—chocolate.

And yet the concentration of culinary activities in two main places did not resolve the problem of getting around. Equipment could always be modernized with new trammels and jacks; enlarged kitchens henceforth had two fireplaces in order to meet the demands of court suppers (which, it might be recalled, generally included twenty-eight dishes served in four courses—soups, roasts, side dishes, and dessert and fruit—although in practice the number of dishes might be doubled or tripled in order to honor the monarch on feast days). Yet these dishes were systematically required to run a kind of "obstacle course," all the more striking in a château like Versailles, which was not subject to urban constraints. Meals started on the ground floor of the southern wing,

Above: The kitchen at the Royal Pavilion in Brighton in 1826. Royal kitchens could rival factories in terms of size, organization, and techniques. The great chef Carême, who cooked for many monarchs including George IV of England, described the slavish work in such kitchens: "Some twenty cooks performing pressing tasks came and went, acting with alacrity in that pit of heat . . . Everyone moved promptly in this inferno, and not a breath was heard—only the chef had the right to make himself heard, and all obeyed his voice. Finally, our suffering became even more extreme when, for nearly half an hour, the doors and windows were closed so that air would not cool the prepared dishes."

where the kitchens reserved for royal service already numbered some twelve rooms packed around a ridiculously narrow cross-passage, as though the principle of having "houses within the house" was sacrosanct. The dishes then had to cross a street, climb the palace stairway and traverse the guards' rooms before they reached the king's first antechamber. This arrangement was designed and built between 1682 and 1685, which means that the court system was already well established and the number and frequency of meals was easily assessed. So the obstacle course was deliberate—courtiers were expected to witness the passage of prepared dishes (and no longer the preparation, as was the case earlier in the century) hidden by their covers (still the same sys-

tem) as they paraded in procession like a piece of royal symbolism. The kitchen remained in the wings, and the cook was less important than the butler or head steward who orchestrated the whole affair.

But Versailles was a contradiction that only the king of France could measure up to. The country's grand families were weary of living in a kind of itinerant state in which the delights of dining and socializing were rationed in parsimonious stages. About 1670–80, when Louis XIV's ascendancy transformed a political ploy into a policing action, the nobility considered returning to Paris and became interested once again in the layout of urban apartments. The bourgeoisie had not waited for the nobility to return, so—given the

Right: George Sand's kitchen in Nohant, France, where nothing has changed since the famous writer oversaw her servants and suppliers in the nineteenth century. "Sometimes I sit at the back of my kitchen and watch the chicken being roasted for dinner, while granting an audience to my rascals and beggars," she wrote to her friend Jules Boucoiran in March 1830. This is also where she made tasty dishes for the likes of Chopin, Flaubert, Balzac, and Delacroix. *Above*: Unlike Nohant, the vast kitchens of aristocratic dwellings in town (and sometimes in the country) had to be placed underground for lack of space. That did not prevent honored guests from occasionally paying them a visit. *Kitchen Interior in a Grand House* by Frank Watkins, 1875.

former group's mimicry of the latter, and everybody's concern for organization—the designs of both groups converged. Hence kitchens migrated once again, first in Paris then in Europe (at that time, France was the sole model). And they would gain, first of all, light. The old sliding windows (filled with "non-opening glass" or "oiled paper") were replaced by swinging casement windows, with handles, which opened in or out and began encroaching on wall space by attaining widths of four or five feet across. In the same spirit, there appeared doors with small glass panes—generally twelve or sixteen—topped by a single-paned, openable window, everything being of "French glass." These provided cooks with some temperature control and above all drew kitchens back to the "social daylight" of the street.

In terms of getting around, a significant transformation occurred in two stages. First, about 1680, the path was shortened by reestablishing the primacy of a straight route over a circuitous one, which brought the kitchen closer to the dining room. Then, about 1700, formal apartments were made distinct from the private apartments (sometimes installed on two different levels), the former devoted to social gatherings and the latter to private life, but both having their own kitchens of relevant size and content. The prototype of such apartments was developed in Paris, then spread to northern Europe about 1710–20: it comprised four rooms in a row, with a hall linking the kitchen to the dining room. Aristocrats also simplified their noble residences when they became interested in cuisine once more; just for fun, they sometimes deigned "to lend a hand, alongside the cooks." The "society apartments" at the château of Trianon drew the kitchens closer to the dining rooms and placed everything on the same floor. The kitchens themselves were reorganized around a square, central room with six doors giving onto the specialized offices aligned in proximity according to order in the meal (the rotisserie was nearest the kitchen, whereas the scullery was stuck beneath two staircases). Louis XV systematized this reorganization by moving the kitchen up to the level of the courtyard terraces; at the same time, the winter dining room of his private apartments was endowed with a prototype of the kitchens that would later be adopted by the bourgeoisie in the nineteenth century: a "main kitchen" which had three sources of heat and fittings along two walls; it was flanked by a larder, itself flanked by the pastry; opposite was the scullery. The butler's pantry served as antechamber to the stairway leading to the apartments.

Eighteenth-century kitchens re-created the family space as personal items were brought in—paintings, stoneware jugs, boxes. Brass was replaced by the more expensive copper. Kitchens were ultimately returning to the center of the household, but they were not yet the focus of family life again. That, however, would be the business of women.

"The kitchen is the only room in the house that we show off to the curious," wrote Abbé Croyer in his 1755 book, *Bagatelles morales*. "Elegance, cleanliness, every kind of convenience—this vast workshop lacks for nothing. It is a masterpiece of modernity in which architecture was pleased to deploy all its resources." *Previous pages*: In the château of Champ de Bataille, Normandy, the private kitchen, restored in a late-nineteenth-century spirit, also serves as dining room. It houses a fine collection of copper molds. *Right*: This new kitchen in a modern house in Buenos Aires was given a deliberately old-fashioned look.

HIER...

1890... Le secret du succès de Tortoni ? Les sorbets qu'il parvenait à servir en plein été ? Il les faisait en utilisant la glace d'un étang de Paris conservée dans un entrepôt spécial nommé "La Glacière". Ce nom est resté attaché à un quartier de la Capitale.

AUJOURD'HUI...

... Pour faire vous-mêmes des glaces, boire frais et conserver les aliments en toute sécurité, il y a aujourd'hui le véritable "FRIGIDAIRE". L'un des 8 modèles de la gamme 1956 répond certainement à vos besoins et à votre budget. Les performances techniques ont fait la réputation mondiale de

FRIGIDAIRE

A partir de 3.500 Frs. par mois.

56 à 60, Avenue Louis Roche
GENNEVILLIERS (Seine) GRE. : 44-50

refrigeration

By keeping produce cool and thus safe to eat, refrigeration has become a crucial feature of modern kitchens. In fact, cold has been domesticated for thousands of years. Recently, however, the increasing infatuation for fresh, healthy food, combined with the proliferation of stickers warning us to "sell by X date" and "store at Y degrees," has meant that the fridge has become the centerpiece of kitchens as well as the most frequently used appliance—in developed countries, a family opens the fridge door, on average, sixty times a day.

Right from ancient times, both the Chinese and the Romans developed various methods for conserving ice, notably storing it in straw-filled trenches in the ground. Even back then, it was used to cool drinks and preserve perishable foodstuffs. Seventeenth-century Europe saw the emergence of "ice chambers," namely underground caves where the winter's natural ice was stored during the summer. In the early nineteenth century, the first ground-level ice houses were built; these rooms had double-lined walls and doors designed along the lines of a ship's ice lockers. By that time, natural ice was already being shipped from Europe to the Caribbean and North America. Household iceboxes, supplied by an iceman who delivered blocks of ice, then spread to homes in major cities. Horse-drawn ice carts could be seen in European streets as late as the 1950s.

A decisive step forward in wider access to cold was made in the early nineteenth century with experiments in mechanical refrigeration—the creation of artificial cold—by the American Oliver Evans and the Englishman Michael Faraday. Several ice-making machines were developed in the following decades, including one that amazed visitors to the 1862 International Exhibition in London by producing huge blocks on a nonstop basis.

It was not until the 1920s that refrigerators of a reasonable size and price were offered to the general public, steadily replacing the old iceboxes. In Paris, the first "refrigerating chest"—dubbed a Polaire—was presented at the 1924 Ideal Home Show. Two years later, the American firm Delco-Light & Co. launched a model that would become the name of a brand known round the world—the Frigidaire.

Artificial refrigeration has been present in kitchens for less than a century. As recently as the 1950s, icemen would deliver blocks (*left*) for the old household iceboxes (*above*, a catalogue illustration for a French icebox, 1928). *Top left and facing page*: French advertisements for refrigerators dating from the 1930s and 1950s.

In the postwar period, refrigerators—especially American—began to incorporate the first freezers, that is to say compartments that maintained temperatures as low as 0°F (–18°C). Separate freezers appeared about 1955, and became common in the following decade, along with the spread of frozen foods, a new culinary revolution. By 1972, some makers were proposing models that cooled down to –25°F (–32°C), which made it possible for people to freeze their own prepared food and dishes. That same year, fridges with automatic ice dispensers appeared on the market. Ten years later, with the development of a compartment maintaining a cool, cellar-like temperature, housewives were offered the luxury of a three-door fridge.

In fact, refrigerator manufacturers have never stopped improving their products, offering temperatures ever more accurate and controlled, appliances less polluting (gas and standard coolants destroy the earth's ozone layer), quieter, and more energy efficient. These days fridges defrost automatically, monitor humidity, and guarantee that a freezer stays cold even during an electrical blackout. Fans now distribute cold air evenly, establishing a uniform temperature that extends the shelf life of food even longer. One Korean manufacturer offers a door in liquid crystal that becomes transparent at the touch of a button. Many other manufacturers have incorporated a system that signals a poorly closed door. A Swedish firm has designed a model with a built-in computer on the door; the computer not only warns when an item of food, identified by its bar code, is about to reach the limit of its shelf life, it can also log onto the Internet in order to do the shopping. Refrigerators are not only marvels of "smart" technology, they are also becoming an art object targeted by leading designers. After having embodied the cool, linear look of lab-like kitchens in the 1950s, fridges now project a friendly, natural feel, as exemplified by the amazingly curved Oz created by Italian designer Roberto Pezzeta.

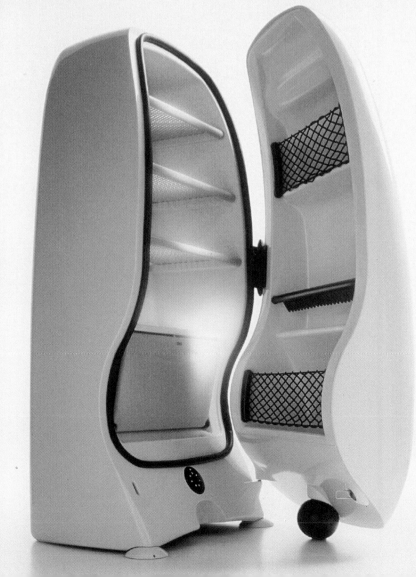

From underground ice chambers to today's sophisticated fridges, the history of refrigeration resembles a hectic race for advances both technical and aesthetic. *Far left, top to bottom*: A 1950s Kelvinator; a high-tech refrigerator in a very masculine kitchen; the handsome Oz fridge designed by Roberto Pezzeta for the Zanussi firm. *Left, top*: An icebox designed by Raymond Loewy for Electrolux in 1939; *left, bottom*: A Gaggenau refrigerator-freezer. *Below*: A SMEG fridge with resolutely 1950s lines.

The Kitchen as Laboratory

This chapter might be titled, "Women Make a Comeback." The development occurred throughout the nineteenth century, coinciding with a great return to private life, almost as though wife and kitchen together became the focus of a house of smaller dimensions. Previously, the presence of women in kitchens had long been suspect; masters of 1700 accused female servants of "taking a bit on the side," meaning that they made extra money by falsifying accounts, by taking commissions on household purchases (a practice that would have induced them to be disorganized, making it easier to lose or break material that would then need replacing), by pretending to lose the shopping money, or even by buying roasts that were deliberately too fatty (since the dripping that fell into the roasting pan was theirs by right). On top of these allegations, women had a poor reputation as cooks—they were either asked to prepare simple dishes requiring a grill or single pot, or else were assumed to be gifted for stews and broths (by association of mater-nal generosity with filling food). Finally, it was not "chic" to employ a woman at the oven. A society lady would make an appearance in the kitchen just to check on the preparation of a meal or to pass the time by whipping up a pot of hot chocolate.

It required a series of chance circumstances for women to regain the kitchen and modify its organization. One economic circumstance occurred about 1750–70, when household lifestyles were cut back as other expenditures became more appealing. People then began recognizing that "a woman's chief skill lay in turning everything to good account." Thus *La Cuisinière bourgeoise*, published by Menon in 1746, offered a series of economic tips to middle-class housewives: a clever cook would use her meat-pie pastry for her pâtés, employ a wide range of implements to avoid pointless expenditure, and above all be careful to "vary the appearance of a table setting." A technical circumstance then inspired progressive minds such as Count Rumford, who in 1798 published an essay on *Heat as a Form of Motion*,

A triple evolution significantly modified kitchen space in the nineteenth century: it became smaller, had to confront a growing concern for hygiene, and increasingly welcomed the presence of women (even in grand households). These new developments eventually led to the twentieth-century kitchen—functional, practical, clean, and light. The first steps toward a functional kitchen can be detected (*left*) in Félix Valloton's *Kitchen Interior with Figure* (or, *The Cook*, 1892) and (*above*) in this illustration of an affluent French kitchen about 1880. *Page 110*: This kitchen unit by the Bulthaup firm is a fine example of contemporary design.

and then went on to offer practical advice on controlling heat sources in order to limit waste due to thermal variance. Since "more fuel is frequently consumed in a kitchen-range to boil a tea-kettle, than, with proper management, would be sufficient to cook a good dinner for fifty men," Rumford devised a roasting oven that cooked very well at much less cost. Closed ranges of this type became so popular in Great Britain that they became known as "Leamingtons," named after a major manufacturer who was located in Leamington Spa. Technical versatility created the function. All these factors led to the reduction and rationalization of kitchen space, entailing the specialization of objects, places, and activities, "each one being suited to the use made of it." Smallness became fashionable, although it is worth recalling a few proportions: for castles, the average number of rooms devoted to the kitchen and its offices went from over twenty in the early eighteenth century to fifteen by 1780 and to "only" six in 1830; provincial residences went from seven to four, while apartments went from three to two (indeed, sometimes just one room next to storage space of easy access and great capacity). In fact, contrary to popular belief, the hallway

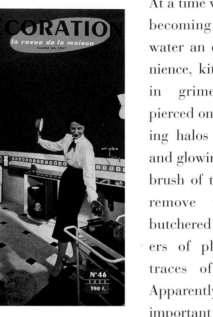

separating the kitchen from the dining room represented a decisive step in bringing kitchen activities back to the heart of the household—the master of the house could henceforth keep an eye on the kitchen and supervise the execution of his instructions.

And what he saw there often made him ill. At a time when energy was becoming cleaner and water an everyday convenience, kitchens wallowed in grime and smoke pierced only by the gleaming halos of copper pans and glowing fire. No quick brush of the broom could remove the blood of butchered meat, the feathers of plucked fowl or traces of ancient soot. Apparently, advice on "all-important hygiene" in the preparation of food, care of utensils, and choice of cloths was falling on deaf ears. With few exceptions, the kitchen remained a kind of stall for doing everything, which wealthier circles preferred to overlook until the mistresses of the house began to poke their noses in the kitchen. And, above all, they began staying there, since male cooks were deserting the hearth in favor of restaurants or the kitchens of a few wealthy profiteers of revolution (industrial or otherwise), where they indulged in extraordinary constructions that rivaled architecture (pastry

Above and right: Two model kitchens dating from 1955. The "laboratory kitchen" concept reached its pinnacle in the 1950s, but the principles had been elaborated a century earlier. Many reformers of the day combined notions of hygiene with Taylorist productivity. The relative smallness of modern spaces came to their aid insofar as it spared the mistress of the house pointless movement and action. The American Catherine Beecher was a pioneer in this sphere. Her conception of the kitchen, described in *The American Woman's Home* (1869), was based on a ship's galley, where the cook only has to take one step to reach everything required.

castles by Marie-Antoine Carême, the greatest pastry chef of the past two centuries, outdid Chalgrin's Arc de Triomphe). Pastry-chef-cum-artists subjected their crews to dreadful working conditions for the glory of creating a fleeting work of art. They had to work "in a pit of heat . . . where everyone moved promptly, [where] not a breath could be heard, and [where] our suffering became even more extreme when, for nearly half an hour, the doors and windows were closed so that air would not cool the prepared dishes. That is how we spent the finest years of our lives." Carême was cooking for history, but the dominant bourgeoisie had little desire to visit a gastronomic pantheon every day. It sought a cuisine which reconciled sight and smell, favored a straightforward association of tastes, and retained hearty textures that reflected the cost of the produce placed on the table. Rather than masculine extravagance, they were happy with essential, feminine, everyday fare.

Women's reconquest was bolstered by hygienists and architects, who wanted kitchens to be lighter, airier, and of sufficient size to function as a "livable space." Kitchens in Tuscany seemed to offer a late-eighteenth-century model in the way they combined space with strength.

Since apartments offered little opportunity to achieve this ideal, adaptations were devised. The coolness required of a kitchen led architects to place it on the north side and to install high, small windows that were always left open (and often covered with a metal screen rather than glass). Having thus "solved" the problem of steam and heat, reformers then attacked dirty floors. About 1780–1810, floors paved with uneven flagstones began to be replaced by a smooth paving of mortar, lime, and cement that could be thoroughly washed with water. Such floors were slightly inclined, making it easy to flush the water down a drain.

Kitchens had not yet attained perfect cleanliness, though. In the mid-nineteenth century, doctors and social reformers joined hygienists in denouncing the fetid atmosphere of kitchens, thought to "breed in cooks the germs of illnesses that will develop later"—an allusion to tuberculosis, that scourge of the century. Everyone offered a solution: architects advocated straight, smooth walls (because "ledges are garbage collectors"), which meant filling holes and cracks and checking windows (ultimately leading to the insulation of kitchens); hygiene specialists, meanwhile, suggested polishing the surfaces that were hence-

Left and above: Kitchens in the 1950s. The point of saving time and motion was to liberate women from daily chores. The same goal spurred architects, starting in the 1920s, to design kitchens inspired by train-carriage kitchens. L–shaped and U-shaped plans became the norm, especially in the 1950s with the rising trend of eating meals in the kitchen once again. "Everything has to communicate, everything has to be functional—no more secrets, no mystery, everything is organized, everything is clear," wrote philosopher Jean Baudrillard. Kitchens henceforth had tile or linoleum floors, and electric appliances reigned supreme.

forth smooth, in order to avoid the build-up of an "organic, dark, damp, and unhealthy compound"; social reformers, backed by engineers, advised using a smooth concrete that would eliminate the cracks in the floor. These ideas began to be applied to the pioneering, low-cost housing built in the late nineteenth century, especially in Germany. Here health considerations dovetailed with social concerns: women had to be "prevented" from leaving their kitchens to join the labor market, where they would create a glut leading to lower wages and

unemployment. Furthermore, a woman content to work in the kitchen would spend much less money buying prepared food in specialized stores. It is therefore not surprising that socialists such as August Babel advocated "sending women to roll up their sleeves in the kitchen," keeping them there thanks to the appeal of the "kitchen of the future, the one seen at the Universal Exposition in Chicago" in 1893.

Indeed, American influence reinforced all these initiatives. It was partly the product of curiosity, of course, linked to the impact in

Above: "The kitchen of the future" as envisaged at an Ideal Home Show in Toronto in 1954. Electric appliances owe their triumph to the arrival of plastic in the 1950s. Formica met with success at the same time, introducing color into kitchens. Designers began taking new interest in kitchen items and furnishings. A concern for attractiveness—for new shapes—became as important as practicality and sturdiness.

Europe of the early skyscrapers, seen as temples to a new way of life adapted to industrialized society. Yet this influence also represented European awareness of a movement that had begun on the other side of the Atlantic thirty years earlier. In 1869, Catherine Beecher was already worried about the repercussions of the migration of servants toward industry, which represented more social upheaval following a Civil War that had permanently disorganized the mobility and labor of individuals. In her book, *The American Woman's Home* (co-written, not coincidentally, with her sister Harriet, author of *Uncle Tom's Cabin*), Beecher reorganized the layout of middle-class homes by giving the kitchen a central place. It once again became the core of everyday life, wedded to the dining room next door. Economy of effort was the first argument put forward, but in fact Beecher was also advocating a redistribution of space according to a binary division between reception area and sleeping zone. This arrangement meant that a single individual could oversee culinary tasks and also occupy her place at the table.

A best-selling book, however, does not make a social revolution. Yet if it fulfills public expectations to such a point that people seize the book's ideas and use them as a political argument, then things may change. That was the opportunity presented to Christine Frederick in the 1910s, when she argued for greater efficiency in the kitchen in the name of the American feminist movement. At a time when the country prided itself as a model for other democracies, how could American women remain slaves to poorly conceived household tasks? Frederick's argument carried all the more weight in that she offered a ready solution, namely applying Taylor's assembly-line methods to the organization of the culinary world. It was a clever suggestion in a country which was just enjoying the successful application of Taylor's ideas in Ford car factories, and in which an unknown stenotypist became a media star by pulverizing the world speed-typing record after having followed the "Taylor method" for a mere matter of months. When it came to kitchens, the method rested on four principles: improvement of tools, specialization of tasks, and fragmentation and rational organization of execution. Frederick began with washing the dishes. By modifying her movements, she was able to save some fifteen

Prior to the economic boom of the 1960s, this concern for style nevertheless remained the privilege of the few. Filmmaker Edward Dmytryk and his wife are seen here in their London apartment, after being forced to leave the United States by the McCarthy witch-hunts.

minutes; by studying kitchen floor plans, she showed that better design would save ten minutes. Her secret was to vary the rhythm by alternating rapid motions with slower ones. Having obtained widespread notice, Frederick went on to broach an idea as vague as it was fashionable: the functional kitchen. She rejected the notion that ample size made a kitchen more convenient, arguing that the important thing was to have a square, well-lit room where the shelves and cupboards are carefully located. Frederick's astonishingly simple suggestion represented an application of Catherine Beecher's basic principle—the kitchen should be divided on the basis of two distinct tasks, preparing the meal and putting clean items away.

As to the battle for hygiene, Frederick attacked on two fronts. First, she was obsessed with eliminating the smell of cold fat and old food, which in certain minds was the distinctive sign of a talented chef; employing the medical arguments of unhealthy air in poorly designed kitchens, she suggested installing extractor hoods, ventilators, and other fanning systems. Next, Frederick felt that a kitchen should be as clean as a hospital: furniture should be washable, which implied the use of metal or then-revolutionary plastic; the floor should be tiled; the walls in ceramics; the ceilings, doors, and window frames painted in washable gloss paint. In one sense, Frederick was proposing a sterile kitchen. Even the utensils were expected to be ergonomic: pots were to be broad but low, with a flat bottom, in order to economize on heat; appliances that could perform repetitive tasks should be chosen. As to the pressure cooker, a modern and economic version of the all-purpose pot, Frederick hailed it as good value for money and gave it pride of place.

Europeans had greater difficulty applying Miss Frederick's tenets, however, since in 1914 less than two percent of English homes had electricity, and France and Germany lagged far behind even that modest figure. By including households where access to electricity was feasible, the figure only rose to a paltry six percent. European notions of comfort and convenience stopped at the kitchen door. Larousse's famous French *Dictionnaire* had a three-column entry on "convenience" without once referring to kitchens. Progress therefore occurred via apparently minor innovations, changes in one detail after another in terms of storage facilities and especially equipment.

Today's "laboratory kitchens" fortunately incorporate what they formerly lacked, the warmth of natural materials. *Previous pages*: This kitchen designed by the German firm SieMatic succeeds in tempering the coolness of steel with highly modern touches of wood (golden maple) and granite. Other contemporary features include transparent cupboards and retro-style appliances. *Left*: A kitchen in Turin, Italy. *Above*: A kitchen in Greenwich Village, New York, where glass cupboards allow for the display of a fine collection of highly colored stoneware from the 1950s.

For example, German designer Peter Behrens, a pioneer of modern architecture, lightened kitchens not only by painting them a daring white but also by introducing AEG's arc lamps, electric kettles, and pots and pans of nickel and aluminum.

World War I acted as a catalyst, less through the destruction of buildings than through the demands of returning "doughboys," who wanted a job and a roof above all. Since these demands were officially recognized by government leaders such as Lloyd-George in Britain, Clemenceau in France, and Orlando in Italy, the 1920s ushered in an era of public housing. The kitchen was placed at the heart of each dwelling, conceived as the vessel of the new life envisaged by progressive doctors and architects. Indeed, kitchens were expected to yield spectacular victories over fatigue and illness, thereby demonstrating the benefits of social-welfare policies. It is hardly surprising that this campaign was led by female architects and economists (female doctors being much rarer), since at the end of a war in which their status, roles, and lives were transformed, women were refusing to "go back into the home."

Germany led the way in improved "order and cleanliness," due not only to a war that hit the country particularly hard, but also to concern over social stability following a short-lived revolution and, above all, to a solid tradition of social welfare dating back to Bismarck. In 1923 Walter Gropius, head of the Bauhaus school, unveiled the prototypical Dessau kitchen. Gropius, who had already demonstrated his skill prior to the war by designing sleeper wagons for the German national railways, paved the way for the so-called "functional" kitchen. His kitchen was arranged in an L shape in order to facilitate the "coordination of areas of storage, preparation, cleaning, and cooking, made simpler by work surfaces and appliances all on one level." This approach was adopted the following year in the Frankfurt kitchen designed by Margarete Schütte-Lihotzki for the city's public housing. The construction of such housing had been halted for ten years, so a large number of units needed to be built quickly. Schütte-Lihotzki, who had trained in Vienna during its heyday, was part of a Frankfurt team—headed by Ernst May, the city's chief architect—which was seeking to rationalize living space. The young woman's ideas were notably inspired by railway dining-car kitchens, which had appeared in 1869; their judicious arrangement of work spaces and practical design of furniture allowed them to serve many meals in a confined space.

The Frankfurt kitchen had few appliances: a gas range, a sink, and a *Kochkiste* (food warmer). In fact, furnishings and implements were secondary—the main thing was the application of Taylorist methods to individual kitchens, granting women more time and better health. The kitchen area was thus reduced to minimal dimensions—45 square feet!—allowing the cook to execute four main tasks, to the

The guiding concepts behind today's functional kitchens may vary according to available space. Limited space calls for compactness (*right*, an old Paris building sports a very modern kitchen designed by Patricio Elliss), whereas vast space encourages fluidity and flexibility (*following pages*, a Bulthaup kitchen in a loft). Large city kitchens are now becoming realms of lightness and mobility.

exclusion of all others: clean, prepare, cook, and store. Nor was their any question of anyone other than the cook herself entering the kitchen. Kids were expected to play elsewhere, and it is hard to imagine them sleeping there. Meals were eaten in another room, ostensibly for lack of space but in fact for reasons of hygiene. In this kind of "secret lab," a cook would have every ingredient within easy reach, like a chemist with skillfully arranged test tubes.

Ernst May built four thousand housing units of this type per year throughout the 1930s. The German example was followed unevenly elsewhere, however. The Belgians (with their "cubex" kitchen), the Dutch, and the Swedes were most receptive. Using glass and steel in kitchens meant participating in the building of a modern nation. In 1933, the Dutch firm Bruynzeel asked architect Pieter Zwart to design mass-producible kitchen furnishings suited to the Frankfurt model. The first items were produced in 1936, but the rattling sabers then threatening Europe restricted their circulation for some ten years. For the moment, modern kitchens remained a paper dream on the pages of glossy magazines, or the object of contemplation at exhibitions such as the 1936 Ideal Home Show in London and the Swedish Pavilion at the 1939 World's Fair in New York. Furthermore, an aesthetic of beauty based on usefulness and soberness met with a certain wariness. First of all, it represented an educated bourgeois taste that required space; it also seemed too Germanic at a time when people

preferred to avoid anything that smacked of social regimentation; in southern Europe, meanwhile, people lacked either the money or space to build new apartments. The main reasons behind the meager interest in this new kind of kitchen, however, were cultural. It was felt that the old kitchen/dining room combination fostered family togetherness, respected provincial traditions, and continued to give, in the words of French government minister Louis Loucheur, "completely satisfying results."

In France, advocates of modern kitchens immediately appeared suspect. The leading figure was a "very red" socialist named Jules-Louis Breton. A disciple of Edouard Vaillant, Breton was an elected official from a bolshevik-leaning district and had been named "Under-Secretary for Inventions" in the wartime government. In short, for the average Frenchman, Breton seemed like a mad scientist with a dagger between his teeth. The second figure was a woman, Paulette Bernège, who had a degree in philosophy, had read Christine Frederick, and wrote a "physiology of habitation" heavily influenced by mid-nineteenth-century utopian thinkers. Bernège launched a "Household Organization League," which made her an agitator as well as a female scholar. Such prejudices fueled the offensive against domestic conveniences as a costly, illusory gratification that would corrupt women and social spirit. For good measure, certain pen-pushers denounced the pernicious influence of slick Protestantism, itself a harbinger

Right: The rectilinear coldness of modern kitchens has been softened by the creativity of architects and interior decorators. In this kitchen designed by architect Marc Corbiau in Ostdunkerke, Belgium, the space is animated by felicitous surprises such as a curved work surface and a piece of salvaged machinery (a professional ham slicer).

of decadence, as seen in Bernège's main key to organizing modern kitchens: piping. Bernège advocated one pipe to extract air, another to purify it, and still others to supply water and electricity, and to flush away garbage. At times, her texts read like a Hergé comic book featuring the American millionaire, Pump, obsessed with speed and pipes.

The "modernists" therefore had a lengthy job ahead of them educating the public. This was also true in the U.S., where the Machine Deco style, inspired by New York's skyscrapers as viewed by designers Paul Frankl and Kem Weber, sparked a good deal of skepticism about "these guys who think a refrigerator can be beautiful." The first stage in that education therefore involved convincing women that a modern kitchen would "save time, money, and space." It was supposed that such women enjoyed a certain financial independence, had other pleasures in life than cooking, and would be attracted to whatever made them stand out from other women in terms of style or color. Also targeted were women whose status and income were upwardly mobile due to their own careers or to the social rise of their "executive" husbands. The second stage entailed interesting husbands in the project by making it part of an overall remodeling of the home and by a timeless appeal to nationalistic pride. Thus the promoters of the first Parisian Ideal Home Show, which opened on October 18, 1923, boasted of the "worldwide" impact as well as the originality and variety of the items on show. The results were mixed, since the 100,000 visitors showed interest in bathrooms, dining rooms, and even the "cubist dream house," but little in electric appliances which implied "that you needed a slave to make a meal." It was not until the years 1927 and 1928 that France's Ideal Home Show drew 400,000 and 600,000 visitors respectively, fascinated by German and American products. The conversion occurred in three stages: initially the French jeered at the "fashion-driven aesthetic of nothingness" (1923–25), then they merely criticized the people who bought German or American products ("Nuremberg lamps" and other appliances with clean lines, angular precision, "aerodynamic" looks) and finally, starting in 1928–29, they began to copy and promote the aesthetic, as though the simple lines promised equally simple relationships between people, too.

Kitchens began to overcome visual reticence to modernity. Even the governments of England and France demonstrated interest in an attitude that "eliminated cumbersome details and offered the joys of cleanliness and organization to the greatest number." To wit, an administrative recommendation in a low-cost housing law passed by the French government in 1928 stipulated that the family kitchen should be divided into two parts: "one, rectangular, unencumbered by any culinary or household appliance, where the family can remain during the day; the other, a kind of well-lit and aired alcove, will be organized

Left: All culinary professionals agree that efficient lighting is a key element of good kitchens. Architect Giovana Gionnattasio took this precept into account when designing her kitchen in Milan. She works on a large, yellow, laminated table designed for everyday meals. The transparent chairs were designed by Philippe Starck.

with the greatest care to reduce the housewife's fatigue to a minimum." In other words, part-time Taylorism had arrived.

This was a long way from the daily litany known to Breton peasants: "Church, chop, chicken, clear up—and that's on Sunday!" In the space of one generation, a complete shift in values had taken place; whereas the word "household" or "culinary" used to be stressed, now people were concerned purely with the "art." This development was spurred by a new appreciation for folklore (at a time when folk art and traditions were coming to the fore as a convenient way of establishing a link between the home of yesterday and the machines of today), by a

magical fascination with the mysterious realms of applied science and art (the incomprehension and later subversion of Marcel Duchamp's "ready-mades" contributed a great deal to this), and finally by the metaphorical sleight-of-hand exploited by every generation (newspapers used images of early potato mashers to illustrate the intricate mesh of diplomatic and political situations in the 1930s, putting culinary and social pulp on the same footing). Similarly, advertisements and articles on the qualities of stoves

(and, later, refrigerators) stressed the importance of "solidity" as a rampart and protection again corruption that clearly extended beyond the kitchen. In a sense, the kitchen-as-lab—light and airy, with clean work surfaces on which the least spot shows, making decorative frills inappropriate—was a democratic kitchen.

The victory of democratic nations in World War II made it easier for this culinary ideology to conquer postwar Europe. French president Henri Queuille inaugurated the 1949 Ideal Home Show in Paris by advocating the "taste, moderation, and cultivation" represented by the new appliances and furnishings. This conquest was short-lived, however, since within the decade families were beginning to weary of a private world that certainly seemed safe yet was so similar to all others in its clean organization that they were thinking of altering it. It was also a long and costly time in coming, as though kitchen cupboards and furnishings "truly held their own" against the intrusion of the modern world—the consumer society—considered vulgar with its garish orange colors, superficial in its taste for detail (down to the tiniest utensil), flighty in its quest for the light-

Right: This kitchen was tailor-made for a demanding, cordon bleu cook. The placement of work surfaces in relation to heat, refrigeration, and water reflects the working reflexes of the mistress of the house. But the key concept behind the design was still "pleasure"—the pleasure of preparing dishes with efficient, handy tools, the pleasure of creativity thanks to utensils that seem to have a soul (like the professional oven of ageless design which generates a timeless feel). *Above*: A kitchen unit by the Bulthaup company.

ness of things, and above all dangerous in its weird idea of advocating automatic appliances. "Automatic" meant there was no more need for an individual's skills and supervision, so that these new kitchen items were "servants" that no longer truly "served" the cook—perhaps technology with its own mysteries and rites would get the better of humans in a new version of the rebellion of objects. And yet by the mid-1960s, kitchens were already "abandoning" the lab in order to return to the family fold. The technology of an object counted less than its style, adapted to the social image of the inhabitants. Sturdiness counted less than price and appearance. It was almost as though, on finally reaching the general public, the kitchen had dismissed its four godparents—doctor, hygienist, engineer, and architect.

Nowadays, the "lab" concept rejects all conformity and uniformity. Although good management of time and space remains crucial, the overall spirit may vary radically depending on an architect's creativity or a user's taste, as illustrated by the two contemporary kitchens shown here. *Above*: This kitchen in Belgium was conceived as a mobile module. Set on a gliding rail, it closes into an egg-shaped cell within which the owner retreats with delight. *Right*: Designed by Bulthaup, this kitchen remains completely open both to light and to visitors.

a chef's kitchen

4

Great chefs in charge of restaurant kitchens—huge machine rooms filled with delectable smells—manage the "mealtime rush" with a mastery that almost seems magical. Once back home in their own kitchens, they like to find the basic qualities of the workplace, which means good equipment—not necessarily sophisticated, but complete and efficient—conveniently arranged in the room. Yet they also want to enjoy something lacking in their workshop-labs, namely a certain comfort, a harmonious setting with a view of nature, and friendly furnishings. The quest for a certain hedonism was stressed by almost all the great chefs who were kind enough to answer our prying questions about their private kitchens. At home, they want to forget that cooking is work.

Setting "My kitchen is in the country—or almost—on the edge of town and above it, on a hill facing a large Romanesque bell tower," writes Georges Paineau, chef at La Bretagne in Questembert, Brittany, in his skillful, storyteller's style. "It is all glassed in, a little like an artist's studio; it overlooks trees, which is a change from the large windowless kitchens in restaurants. I'm not in a hurry here, I'm not tense, there's no 'quasi-athletic' sprint during the mealtime rush. Instead, there's a serene and humble attitude toward what has been my job for thirty years. As I monitor simmering pots I can watch the birds playing in the yard, swirling around the trees. It's a real pleasure to finally spot the crested tit (no less) discovering the ball of suet and seeds that I have lovingly set out for him the past two winters. But then a buzzer pulls me back into line and, like the little bell that stops catechism kids from whispering, reminds me of the task at hand!"

A similar, nearly religious feeling—born not only of the bell of the timer but probably also that of the Romanesque church—was expressed by **Marc Meneau** (chef at L'Espérance in Saint-Père-sous-Vézelay, Burgundy): "The privilege of living opposite the basilica in Vézelay inspired me to install a large glass window overlooking the basilica. While at mass in the kitchen, I can hear another one in the basilica." What seems to count most for chefs is—unlike their windowless professional kitchens—to have an opening on the world, a contact with nature. Answering our questions at a time when he was renovating his house and designing a new kitchen, the main goal of **Jean-Michel Lorain** (La Côte Saint-Jacques, Joigny, Burgundy) was to have "a light kitchen, with a wide view of the outside, and sufficiently spacious to receive my friends." The same concern to communicate

All good cooks, professional or amateur, dream of direct contact with nature. The kitchen of the Troisgros restaurant in Roanne, France, (*left*, seen during the "rush hour") is a vast room drenched in light during the day, thanks to a large window overlooking the herb garden. At home, Michel Troisgros has established the same link between kitchen and herb garden.

with the exterior was expressed by the late **Richard Olney**, a peerless chef who wrote many books on wine and gastronomy from his home in Provence, where he chatted shortly before he passed away. "My kitchen opens onto a terrace. For five months of the year, we eat under the trellis." Again, the ideal kitchen for **Emile Jung** (Au Crocodile, Strasbourg) should be "light and spacious, open to the exterior, designed with noble and sturdy materials that can stand the test of time and use." The same concern, combined with the idea of taking advantage of nature's bounty, is apparent in the very handsome house of the great Chinese-American chef **Ken Hom** in Quercy, southwest France: "My kitchen spills into the garden, which makes it ideal for cooking since I can gather fresh herbs." In the home of **Michel Troisgros** (Maison Troisgros, Roanne), the kitchen "opens wide onto the dining room (no door), and also onto the outside, in order to take advantage of the natural light. It is at ground level and gives onto a small herb garden."

Olivier Roellinger (Les Maisons de Bricourt, Cancale, Brittany) recently moved into a new home and has only a modest kitchen for the moment. But his dream kitchen sums up the aspiration for well-being. It would be a kitchen "facing the ocean, the open sea, with the waves breaking down below, so that on stormy days the spray would hit the little window panes. Behind the house there would snuggle a little vegetable garden in the form of a mosaic of squares separated by pebbles from the beach. In the cool, damp cellar, a system of canals would draw the sea, at high tide, into a pool where various lobsters and crabs would await our gastronomic cravings."

When overlooking and communicating with nature are not key features of a kitchen—or when made impossible by an urban environment—chefs nevertheless try to evoke nature through clever tricks. It is truly present in the personal kitchen of the typical Burgundian home of **Bernard Loiseau** (La Côte d'Or, Saulieu) which, in addition to a large window,

Whether full-time chef or not, the most enthusiastic cordon bleu cooks use professional equipment. *Below*: This Parisian cook is an amateur herself, but her equipment is worthy of one of the smaller grand restaurants. *Bottom*: As to Provençal chef Roger Vergé, when at home he wants to forget the frenzy of his restaurant, the Moulin de Mougins, yet he still employs the finest tools when preparing a meal for family or friends. *Right*: The Dehillerin store in Paris is a veritable museum of kitchen utensils, and has been supplying professionals and amateurs the world over since 1920.

boasts "authentic, warm materials of wood and stone." Meanwhile, **Alain Passard** (Arpège, Paris) has managed to re-create at home the space and light conducive to the kind of serenity offered by nature: "For me, a kitchen is above all a place of silence and receptiveness. When designing my personal kitchen, I considered the transparency of the furnishings and the lightness of the place—the furnishings are in very pale sycamore and the work surfaces in green English slate." Space and light are once again the main characteristics of London gourmet **Terence Conran**, the man who revolutionized the art of furnishing homes (Habitat, The Conran Shop) and who owns several restaurants. "In London, my open-plan kitchen is drenched in light, allowing me to cook, eat and live there, which encourages conversation and participation. When we have guests to dinner, the cook isn't banished somewhere else."

Organization Since great professionals do not like to waste time with pointless movements or operations, most chefs are as demanding of their private kitchens as they are of their workplace. These demands were summed up simply and lucidly by **Roger Vergé** (Le Moulin de Mougins, Mougins, near Cannes): "An easy kitchen is a well-organized kitchen, where everything is within reach." Ken Hom offers a specific lesson on this matter: "A kitchen should be practical. I like to have pots, pans, and woks there, within reach, easy to grab when necessary. The sink should also be placed nearby, so that dishes can go straight from the preparation stage to the oven. The fridge is also nearby. My knives are kept near the oven, allowing me to cut, slice, and dice without having to run very far. The fridge, oven, and sink are close together to make preparation easy, whereas the dishwashing corner is further away, because I don't like to mix the cooking and the washing up."

Left: People who like great food turn their personal kitchens into little temples, private yet ritualistic. Who would dare disturb the highly organized disorder of Ken Hom's kitchen? This great Chinese-American chef has a house in southern France where he receives friends such as Tony Blair. Although as hedonistic as Hom, Englishman Terence Conran likes spacious, light kitchens that open onto greenery, as seen first in his apartment in London's Docklands (*below*) and again in his country home in Barton Court (*bottom*). Such a kitchen is "the only room you really need," claims Conran.

Marc Meneau's kitchen is also perfectly organized. "Since I have a room ten feet wide by twenty-three feet long, I divided it into two parts. One part is storage—a refrigerator for liquids and cheese, a dishwasher, a sink, draining rack, food cupboard, and cupboard for plates and glasses. The other part is technical—a stove with four burners, a simmering plate, two ovens and a slow-burning stove, a convection oven with fan, a cooling tray and a large marble work surface, underneath which is a fridge for food products and storage space for cooking vessels. Above the work surface are two marble shelves, ten feet long, which hold an assortment of cooking condiments as well as a display of old cooking utensils. Everything is lined with marble slabs to make it easy to clean splatters. The space between the work surface and the stove is just three feet wide, so the cook merely has to turn around to get from work surface to oven."

Emile Jung's "ideal kitchen" would feature the most logical pathways possible. "What counts is the arrangement of surfaces, which then conditions everything else: efficient use of time and space, ease of movement, economy of operations. Thus, at the entrance to the kitchen I'd put a surface for setting down the produce, with a nearby sink for washing it. Next, a fridge for storing the produce. Next to that, a work surface would make it easy to operate and therefore stimulate creativity. Following from there, logically, would come the cooking zone. And finally, I'd have another work surface for carefully dressing the dishes for presentation."

Like Jung, Troisgros, and Passard, all of whom insist on having a good extractor hood, Meneau stresses the importance of good ventilation in a family kitchen "to prevent kitchen smells from invading the other rooms in the apartment." Finally, Jung adds an indispensable element to the proper organization of a kitchen: "One more detail—lighting. It's crucial above each work surface with, if possible, daylight bulbs to avoid mistaking true colors and shapes. Back-lit surfaces should be corrected with artificial lighting to prevent bother and fatigue."

Equipment All great chefs have their own personal kind of genius, their own obsessions and techniques. Thus their opinions may diverge when it comes to tools. All, however, stress the crucial importance of the quality of cooking appliances. "The most important thing in a kitchen," writes Roger Vergé, "is first of all an excellent oven, a multifunctional one with convection fan, sufficiently large. I favor electricity with a ceramic stove-top and an additional, Japanese-style snack burner." Olivier Roellinger pictures an ideal kitchen as having two heat sources: "Along the main wall would be a fireplace with a large wood-burning rotisserie; somewhat to the side would be a big AGA, giving off its gentle heat all day long, especially in the morning, plus two large, hot burners for the wok and for cooking shellfish." Troisgros uses "two types of heat: very hot gas for searing, and four electric infra-red zones for slow cooking. The oven is multifunction, my favored type. It is essential that it heat up to 630°F (333°C), notably for pizzas." Bernard Loiseau, meanwhile, has opted for equipment as complete as it is traditional: "In the fireplace I've put a Lacanche oven, completely manufactured just a few miles from Saulieu. It's their Fontenay model with electric convection oven, deep fryer, plate-warmer, grill, two burners and a gas 'rush' burner. Its black color and brass trim go perfectly with the family atmosphere of the kitchen. My wife also wanted to have two induction burners, which are less dangerous for the kids and easier to clean." Like Madame Loiseau, almost all chefs have opted for induction burners at home. Georges Paineau praises "their flexibility and ease of care." **Jacques Chibois** (La Bastide, Saint Antoine, Grasse) is equally enthusiastic about them: "I especially use induction for pastry and hors-d'œuvres. It's much more flexible and twice as fast as gas and electricity. It means cooking without heat, without dirt, without grease. It's a perfect way to cook in a domestic kitchen, the greatest revolution in kitchens in the past twenty years!" A number of cooks are also equipped with a grill, such as

Georges Paineau and Richard Olney, while Jean-Michel Lorain dreams of "a traditional charcoal grill, for unparalleled cooking." As for Alain Passard, he could not do without the perfect oven: "It's the luxury item in my kitchen, very big and deep, with an excellent spit and above all a stone for baking bread."

Chefs are naturally accustomed to using the finest equipment, and are unhappy with cheap tools at home. "I tend to buy professional equipment for the kitchen because it's tougher, lasts longer, and gives a professional touch to the kitchen," admits Ken Hom. In the kitchen in his old Provençal house, Richard Olney used "traditional equipment—wrought iron meat and fish grills for the fireplace, marble mortar and pestle, earthenware gratin dishes, stew pots and casserole dishes; copper pans, saucepans, deep and shallow frying pans, and bowls; then come the special omelet pan, crepe pan, and small implements (hand grinder, vegetable slicer, some thirty knives), etc." Roger Vergé offers a more concise list of absolutely essential material. "You need to have: a set of stainless steel pans; cast-iron saucepans with lids (Le Creuset type); at least two sinks with hot and cold water for washing vegetables and other things; a toaster that can also serve as warmer; a multifunction mixer/blender; a selection of small implements (basic tongs, wooden spatulas); a small dishwasher with a quick cycle." Terence Conran eschews the superfluous. "An excellent set of saucepans and a selection of pots, a few sharp knives, a

Right: All chefs seek a serenity that is not always easy to find in the workplace. "For me, a kitchen is above all a place of attentiveness and silence," says Alain Passard, seen in his Arpège kitchen. A restaurant kitchen, however, is a special place enlivened with a certain dose of madness. In his famous play *The Kitchen*, Arnold Wesker wanted to stage this madness (*top right*). "If all the world's a stage for Shakespeare," he comments, "for me it's a kitchen."

cutting board and wooden spoons. I hate gadgets, and can't understand why people clutter up their workspace and cupboards with electric gizmos that they rarely—if ever—use."

Georges Paineau is not one of those people. A quick glance at his kitchen produced a witty list: "Three small whisks and at least four ladles, a mixing bowl and two salad bowls, three forks including one for roasting, a knife sharpener and the garden shears (which don't really belong here) . . . "

The Joy of Kitchens

"We lived in an apartment in town, with sliding cupboard doors and a kitchen lit by long neon tubes that made it seem like a bathroom. I remember my parents' friends saying, 'Wonderful! Just like the movies!' Then all the adults would rattle off the advertising spiel for the 'Kitchen Comfort' brand, over a jazzy tune— 'If you've always admired lucky American housewives, admire them no longer: thanks to these appliances, you'll stay sexy even while cooking up a storm. You'll welcome your hubby to a cozy little kitchen and your kids will eat with gusto.' And I remember thinking, 'If the ideal kitchen is supposed to resemble a bedroom, then I don't want one.' I didn't really see what all the spotlessness, convenience, efficiency, and everything else implied by the word 'modern' had to do with joy. The appliances promoted by the ads seemed like intruders who had forced my parents to disrupt the arrangement of a normal kitchen—like my grandmother's, for instance—by installing electric plugs here, pipes there, and putting white cubes where the jam cupboard, the meat safe, and the stove used to be. My grandmother had

told me that a kitchen should first be furnished, then decorated—whereas all year long I heard my parents explain the attractions of the appliances they owned while dreaming out loud of the ones they'd buy, like the freezer that could keep the golden cakes you see in the pages of magazines. At every meal, they discussed equipment—it was like listening to my ski instructor. And then, there was always someone who would chip in, 'It's so spotless! You hardly smell a thing. It's heavenly, your kitchen.'"

Personal testimony sometimes documents a period as surely as an archive. The account above constitutes the death certificate of kitchens as they had evolved over four centuries. The first shock is the disappearance of flames and weightiness, a development that took a century via the intervention of gas and then electricity. Early gas flames and electric rings still called for thick, solid shapes. Heavy materials reigned— saucepans made by the likes of Dehillerin inevitably looked as though they had been wrought in Vulcan's forge by some gourmet. Utensils had to protect food from aggressive flames. At the same time, they embodied the

Above: "They wanted to make people forget about eating in the kitchen," wrote novelist Marguerite Duras, "but that's where people gather, where they go when night has fallen, where it's warm and you can stay with mother while she cooks." The author's kitchen on Rue Saint-Benoît in Paris was a long way from "those modern kitchens where people make only steak and French fries," yet Duras would prepare delicious and frequently exotic dishes for her friends here.
Left: Jean Cocteau, on the other hand, made do with a bachelor's "kitchenette" in his apartment at the Palais-Royal.
Previous pages: The kitchen of a mountain chalet in Savoy, built in 1728.

values of a time when grand bourgeois cuisine was elaborated, a century of iron and secret private lives. The kitchen was the refuge—or rather, fortress—of nineteenth-century morality and lifestyle. Objects displayed their metallic skeletons and flaunted their weightiness, as though proving they were not to be counted among the chintzy objects whose place was in the sitting room.

The last third of the twentieth century, meanwhile, was governed by the sign of everything light: light objects that can be handled faster and easier; light forms that reflect a TV culture which inculcates society with a taste for colors and images; light decisions in the face of consumer diversity backed by the gauzy, seductive world of advertising; and finally light people who have rediscovered dieting and disapprove of any weightiness or heaviness in the human body. Gone are the ovens that were placed in an exact spot with the same care as a chest of drawers in the sitting room. Opening a cupboard no longer means discovering a hoard of nourishment, but rather executing a practical task, which explains sliding doors—no one really cares whether they are open or closed.

This revolution has affected the entire inner workings of the sacrosanct preparation of a meal. In order to grasp the scope of it, we need merely recall the slowness with which culinary habits and techniques evolved until the 1950s. In a way, the inventories drawn up by Scappi remained more or less unchanged five cen-

turies later. Tomatoes and potatoes, meanwhile, had both taken two hundred years to find their way onto European plates. Now the culinary fortress has suddenly surrendered. The slow cooking techniques required by cauldron and pot over coals or stove are disappearing, as is the use of water as the basic kitchen element when cooking soups and boiling food. In the Emilia-Romagna region of Italy, families used to alternate polenta, minestra, soup, and pasta, depending on the season or the daily chore to be performed; nowadays, pasta has relegated the other dishes to the role of picturesque walk-ons. The same is true for cakes and their various molds; the latter are slowly evolving into decorative knickknacks now that it is so much easier to buy a standard cake than to bake one.

This brings us to the main reason for the rupture—the obsession with time. It is not just a question of changing from rural time to urban time, because the race against the clock is even affecting our choice of food. On the way out are turnips, beans, and marrows, judged too slow to cook and associated too closely with hearty dishes now considered indigestible. The utensils used to prepare such dishes are disappearing along with them—no more gratin dish for layering potatoes and marrows, no thick-bottomed pan for frying bacon fat, tomatoes, onion, and marrow. Quick, light cuisine breaks with a culinary tradition of respect for a ritual of ingredients dictated by seasonal or liturgical cycles, orchestrated by preparation techniques

Previous pages: The kitchen of the great English food writer, Elizabeth David. Her nephew, designer Johnny Grey, remembers that the table was not only the scene of superb dishes and conversation, but also served as a desk and a work surface. Whereas order reigned in lab-style kitchens, today's user-friendly kitchens encourage improvisation and spontaneity. *Right*: The pleasures of the kitchens of yore have thus been re-created (*right*: château of Fontaine-Française, near Dijon).

adapted either to everyday meals or festive banquets, to Sunday dinners or to wedding and funeral feasts. In Romagna in Italy and Brittany in France, for example, people used a special mold to make cakes for Corpus Christi or the Procession of Saint Yves. This traditional system was reinforced by the specialization of artisans, each trade having its particular culinary habits that suited an immutable cuisine.

It therefore took more than a paean to modernism to bring about a new regime so swiftly and so enthusiastically. The kitchen of the 1960s triumphed because it made work go faster, and sometimes better and more cheaply, than a servant; its appliances and organization favored the spread of the bourgeois model of gastronomy, the dream of the burgeoning middle classes. Contrary to popular belief, families were not seeking pleasure so much as the association of scientific progress and industrial quality with status. That explains the simultaneous popularity of Formica and loathing for completely automated objects. The former symbolized a time when everything seemed possible, a time when material seemed to bend and conform—since it was plastic—to human sci-

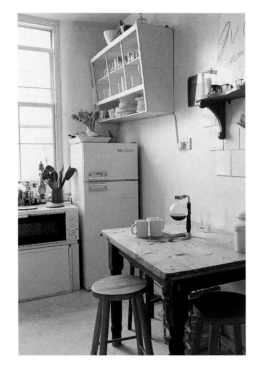

ence. In a new twist, materials were no longer a sign of lasting tradition, but rather of innovation adapted to the constraints of the day in general and of families in particular. Going one step further, objects and furnishings became colored by such ideas—the neutral white of Braun appliances, directly inspired by the Ulm school (the post-1945 heir to the Bauhaus), underscored the material and shape of a kitchen blender that "well-bred people" would recognize as a variation on classical forms; the gleaming steel worked by designers such as Massoni, Mazzeri, and Vitale for the Alessi firm, meanwhile, brought factory techniques to the culinary world by masking the raw aspect of materials, even as their flat, strong colors represented a way of perceiving the surrounding environment.

Even a utensil as familiar as the pressure cooker illustrates these new associations. On one hand, manufacturers respected the tradition of heavy, sturdy, "hand-finished" forms (round and oval) that immediately evoked images of family gatherings around a dish lovingly prepared by a feminine hand. In 1957, for example, the Le Creuset firm marketed a pressure cooker called Doufeu ("gentle

Previous pages: Wood still dominates in hedonistic kitchens, as in this warm kitchen belonging to Michel Biehn, a Provençal antique dealer, decorator, and author of gourmet books. Wood's many shades and textures can create varied effects, respecting local traditions and settings while providing the natural warmth often lacking today. At a time when authenticity is highly valued, wood evokes the kitchens of our ancestors, making a comeback over plastic which had temporarily dethroned it. The London kitchen of artist Joan Hecktermann. *Right*: A kitchen in Punta del Este, Uruguay.

flame"), a barely modified version of the original 1925 model but with a name that underscored, almost redundantly, its culinary vocation. Yet one year later the same company called on designer Raymond Loewy to develop La Coquelle. Loewy made absolutely no technical improvement, but instead concentrated on shape, material, and color. His model was designed to suggest finer cooking, to play a different role on stove and table—it had to pull off the tour de force of making cast iron appear light. The solution was remarkable in its simplicity: perspective was altered by adopting a smaller bottom and molding the top into the shape of a rugby ball. This presented two

advantages, because when placed on the table the pressure cooker projected the reassuring image of a family pot, yet when placed in the oven or in a cupboard it occupied less space and suited the rationalized organization of kitchens. And then there was its epoch-making detail—a heat-proof plastic handle.

In a complementary yet opposite trend, people refused to abdicate control over the preparation, cooking or even cleaning up of a meal. A work-free kitchen was inconceivable. Objects of technical progress were expected to crush and mix—mere domestic chores—but humans wanted to retain the distinctive role of deciding and ordering. Hence the use of

Left: In this house on Long Island, the joy of cooking is enhanced by the view of the yard. And an eye can be kept on the kids as they play while the meal is being prepared. Kitchen chores no longer exclude the cook from the rest of the house and the outside world. *Above*: The link to the outside world is symbolized by the quest for light, epitomized by this Milanese kitchen drenched in light by a tall French door.

machines was still seen as debasing, as though the factory environment was polluting the world of culinary delights. Reconciling these conflicting attitudes required subtle tactics. In the countryside of northern Italy and southern France, for instance, stoves were designed to cook with both flame and electricity. Or traditional locations—such as the fireplace—would be used as the site of modern ovens. Old-fashioned utensils such as mortars were transformed into decorative objects or recipients. The very arrangement of preserves in the cupboard and food in the fridge reflected a desire to reappropriate the rhythm of the markets or seasons. By modernizing and equipping their

kitchens, homeowners showed that they had money and knew how to save time over old methods; by inhabiting their kitchens, they showed that they knew how to use that time, that they had not lost touch with culinary savoir faire. Should anyone have doubted this, advertising was there to remind them. Brandt thus invented a slogan which put technology in its place: "Brandt is part of the family."

So just when the long process of making kitchens more functional and hygienic was nearing completion, about 1975–80, people began to dread a place of mechanical convenience where activities would become repetitive, where smells would be limited to air

Kitchens are becoming the most open space in the home, whether in a renovated farm near Bruges in Belgium (*above*) or a chalet in Montana (*right*). People are rediscovering the friendly atmosphere of a shared space as boundaries are abolished between kitchen, dining room, and living room. This departitioning is due to Frank Lloyd Wright, an architect who did not like walls—it was back in 1934 that he first eliminated a wall between kitchen and dining room.

fresheners, where food would increasingly seem ready-made. Seeking joy in the kitchen then meant fleeing it, meant returning to the disordered trace of yesterday's kitchens, building new ways of experiencing and expressing that place. In other words, technological values had to be converted into principles of sociability. The operation turned out to be tricky, because kitchens had become highly attractive prisons. There was no question, for example, of fleeing via the extractor hood as though it were a chimney; a chimney, once past its throat of soot, led to the sunlight, brought hints of wind or rain, made the flame quiver, established invisible contact with the outside world that provided the ingredients of the meal. A

hood, in contrast, incarnates the triumph of the principle of extraction in the home—it imposes its noise and cleanliness without the least respect for a cook's ears or nose. Just try cooking *faggioli all'uccelletto* in a glazed earthenware pot like the ones used around Pienza: with a throbbing ventilator, it is impossible to hear the subtle bubbling of the beans, to smell the wafts of basil and tomato that make up the very alchemy of the dish.

In fact, a modern kitchen is a room that has

abandoned its own special geometry in favor of an aesthetic of flatness. A kitchen used to be organized somewhat like an ancient temple— the columns of the chimney, andirons, and hanging grills were topped by the entablature of the shelves, everything being focused on the central hearth, itself dedicated to the gods of food. But today's wondrous machines are hidden in ceramic shells, while smooth work surfaces have leveled the niches, corners, and hollows of disparate furnishings. Kitchens now reflect "TV style" in a number of ways. First, the shape of a television corresponds to today's kitchen design—as a square object that is becoming increasingly flat, the television now dominating the kitchen during mealtimes hardly differs from a modern oven, that light object in which glass and electronics have replaced cast iron. Second, the television has become an additional member of the family, an object that demands special attention—adorned in knickknacks, family photos, indeed Christmas tinsel, the TV has become a special shelf to which all family eyes turn. Finally, television floods the kitchen with color, images and advertising that have no immediate relationship to food. For all those reasons, television has

Casual, free, spontaneous spaces can be a stimulus to creativity. In the kitchens of cool city dwellers, roller blades are matched by casters under kitchen units that make everything roll, not just traditional dessert carts and side tables . . .

dynamited the traditional fortress-kitchen, driving people to abandon tried-and-true models, regular timetables, and sovereign nutritional functions.

The kitchen is becoming a game room. And the fun is sweeping away the social morality that originated in Germany and was recycled by East Coast designers in the U.S.—what a *New Yorker* critic described as an extremely Protestant sense of taste so disgusted by bodies that it wanted them spindly, so unhappy with this world that it endowed a toaster with ethical value, and so smug about its social status that even its food was expected to contribute to its salvation. These days, however, kitchens are acquiring dials, functions, and buttons that make technology seem like a big game of outer space reduced to the household universe. This playful side has had the considerable advantage of encouraging men to return to the kitchen, first timidly in the 1970s and now boldly. Man the "creator" (or playing at it) has at long last taken over from man the artisan after a long period of female domination. Amateurs (in every sense of the word) are rediscovering the pleasure of being in the kitchen, the fun of playing with all those buttons and machines.

General Electric's Stratoliner sports a name that sounds like some legendary rock guitar played by Eric Clapton or Jeff Beck, allowing for highly original "harmonies." Sales catalogues boast of the Stratoliner's "jet flow" and "centrifugal clutch" as though describing Batman's oven. Then there is the fun of discovering color combinations that violate the codes which conventional taste was supposed to enforce. White appliances are decking their hospital-like spotlessness with touches of red or blue; brown furnishings no longer enjoy a monopoly on "authenticity" and are rivaled by green, yellow, and gray; black-and-white functionalism has lost its stranglehold on seriousness thanks to kaleidoscopic kitchens.

The colors, patterns, and very asymmetry of these flat forms permitted a transition from the kitchen-as-lab to a kind of synthesized space. For this pantry of pleasure, everyone would poach symbols of well-being from childhood memories, from collages (whether Pop art, family photos or drawings), from comic books, and from construction sets (reworked, if necessary, by the computer). As an example, take the exceptional career of designer Ettore Sottsass, from his first projects for Olivetti in 1961 to his

. . . but also cabinets, storage units, chopping blocks, work surfaces, bottle racks, and even cooking equipment (hot plates and mini-ovens), all of which can be moved at will. Down with everything fitted and built-in, up with the heterogeneous, movable, and flexible! *Above and left*: Movable units by Bulthaup.

1981 launching of the Memphis movement, featuring items such as an asymmetrical Casablanca dresser for storing the dishes of a family as decomposed (or recomposed) as the dresser itself, whose single drawer might hold Madonna knives (proof that sexual fantasies—an old theme in culinary literature—are every diner's indispensable playmates).

Yet the diner has also returned to the kitchen from personal health concerns, yielding what might be called a new version of the kitchen-lab. At a time when men are adopting the female obsession with eternal youth (with all that entails in the way of anxiety and effort), the kitchen has become a lair for concocting elixirs of health and longevity. This supposes new rules: rules for balancing ingredients (of the "more vegetables, less starch" or "lots of chicken" variety), rules for healthy preparation methods (steam cooked, cold pressed, dry grilled or with just a drop of olive oil) and even rules for marketing which provide an opening for pseudo experts who come from nowhere but are good at manipulating masculine frustration, as well as for designers able to devise objects that reflect the complex yearning for "nostalgic," healthy food. Thus the Mama, Enzo Mari's reincarnation of the pressure cooker, is presented as a tribute to maternal cooking, a return to rounded shapes, with a name that rings like a promise of slow-cooked food that never sticks (ever the concern with health). It even incorporates a "modern" detail, because plastic has been replaced by ceramics. This personal and symbolic reappropriation brings the recentering of kitchens to a close. The path was shorter, of course, for people living in the United States and northern European countries which adopted the open-plan kitchen with bar, thereby creating a continuum between living room and kitchen. Yet in all developed countries over the past twenty years, the room devoted to cooking has increased in surface area—roughly ten square feet every seven years—whereas temporary facilities or closet-sized nooks are now the fate of only three percent of residents of major Western cities.

Space is only an enabling condition, but other indications confirm this trend—in 1980, the Ideal Home Show in Paris presented an "extendable kitchen" that corresponds to French habits insofar as one kitchen out of five is the product of do-it-yourself improvements.

Working in an old kitchen with its original decor and utensils means attempting to rediscover old habits, sounds, smells, and tastes. These days, older kitchens are often restored rather than renovated. *Left*: Catherine Sterling's kitchen in Saint-Rémy-de-Provence, with authentic objects including early-twentieth-century saucepans made of aluminite. *Above*: A kitchen designed by Johnny Grey, with furnishings in cherry and sycamore, work surfaces in granite, and a central island for preparing dishes. *Following pages*: An impressive eighteenth-century kitchen all in granite, once the home of poet Teixeira de Pascoaes in northern Portugal, now a hotel which serves traditional cabbage soup accompanied by *vinho verde*, one of the country's fine young white wines.

In the same way, the rate at which kitchen items are replaced had long stagnated at once every four years but now has dropped to eighteen or twenty months in France, thirty months in the rest of Europe. The organization of kitchens today therefore constitutes a complex collage: everywhere the "heritage industry" imposes a nostalgia as artificial as it is indispensable, as uniform as it is conducive to regional specificities. For instance, the 3T series designed in 1968 by Roger Tallon for France has been reissued in Japan, although it now symbolizes the historical influence of aus-

tere Japanese dinnerware on French creativity even as the latter conferred the fame of its brands—in this case, Christofle, Daum, and Ravinet Denfert—on Franco-Japanese kitsch. This kind of development rests on the spread of models based on the well-known trickle-down mechanism: envy and imitation are the best agents for changing habits. It is no longer a question of simply acquiring one more appliance, however, since now an entire dream has to be built with hands in the present and heart in the past. Indeed, the contemporary kitchen is expected to answer a question that obsessed

A taste for the past, which can be found in many modern kitchens, is like a struggle against the ephemeral. This rejection of everything "fast," fleeting, and disposable favors lasting values, the ones which were handed down in the past and can still be passed on. From this standpoint, nothing is more significant than the craze for "old-style" stoves, made by hand in cast iron. The famous British-made AGA stoves (*above*, in London and *right*, in Cambridge) have not changed since they were invented by Swedish Nobel physicist Gustaf Dalen in 1922. Remarkably simple, sturdy, and efficient, AGAs are loved for the steady, gentle heat they impart to the entire house.

twentieth-century individuals: can it dissipate the dread of loneliness and the fear triggered by the vastness of the outside world? That is probably one of the main reasons for the comeback of wood in kitchens. From oak to pine via trompe-l'oeil veneer, wood is now a magnificent unifying theme even as it allows for all kinds of local specificities. In Alsace and Bavaria, for example, built-in cupboards are now being replaced by "old-style" buffets, linen closets transformed into crockery cabinets, wooden benches, and pestles—an ersatz Germanic *stub*, or chamber, satisfying rural and family nostalgia. Paradoxically, this concern to create an intimate ambiance focuses on

a room where shared meals are rarer and ceremonial culinary gatherings are less frequent, notably to the benefit of restaurants. A hypothesis might be put forward: kitchens are seen as the best place to install the family "museum" of souvenirs and heirlooms gleaned from the village or based on oral tradition ("grandma's recipe," "after-dinner tales," regional names for a given dish). It all smacks of illusion, yet works thanks to the magic of communications. By a twist of fate, the very cookbooks, magazines, and television that helped to bankrupt the closed, nonreproducible world of ancient customs henceforth promote unbridled recuperation of traditional

Formerly relegated to the far wing of a château, the kitchen has now returned to center stage. Not only is it the focus of social gatherings and hearty meals, but it also serves as a showcase for personal objects of value, whether retrieved from the family attic, brought back from voyages, unearthed at a flea market, or bought at an art gallery. In this château kitchen owned by Jean-Charles de Castelbajac in Loubersan, southern France, where Saint Anthony watches over the dinner guests, as in many kitchens the room's decor projects an image of what you are—or would like to be—and not what you have.

forms that are no longer authentic but whose "local" or "typical" color seems indispensable to the flea markets that kitchens have become. That is why Provence-style sunny red floor tiles can be matched with "combinable" bric-a-brac ranging from childhood souvenirs and old photos of grandmother's kitchen (country look and Delft tiles included) to kitchen units straight from the illustrated weeklies of the 1960s (featuring shelves now used to store either plates or compact discs, since cooking and storage units are henceforth combined like a stereo system, VCR-style programming buttons included). This collage principle is not much different from the culinary one in our plates, thanks to the internationalization of cuisine and, conjointly, the defense of national identities. The relative dosage of these two tendencies is a question of fashion, which brings us back to the crucial role of media impact: the French remain leading consumers of saucepans, their average set numbering five as against the Germans' two, whereas the British, riding a culinary wave for the past fifteen years, have upped their supply by two, bringing their average set of saucepans to four (thereby equaling the Italians' score). Thanks to culinary celebrities, however, the shape and substance of saucepans have evolved: Americans are beginning to abandon their high, narrow saucepans; stainless steel now covers thick sheet copper that conducts heat perfectly, is easy to clean, and gleams under electric lights. In the end, kitchens are being asked to

restore a sense of gastronomic tradition by offering men and women the power to control this locus of life and sociability. Since ceremonial control is almost extinct and nutritional control has slipped into the hands of manufacturers and doctors (the two groups that dictate and ration modern diets), there only remains control over the decor, the stage set for the theater of mealtime. The visual impact of kitchens now takes precedence over smells and tastes; formerly, the kitchen area was identified through an immaterial, unconscious, sensory attraction—once people entered the kitchen, they lifted lids to inhale the odors, touched food

Stone floor, old chairs, ancient stove, antiques on the walls, exposed beams: the current dream of traditional kitchens is inspired by those of the grand houses of yore (*above*, a kitchen put together entirely from salvaged material). It is the antithesis of the functional, interchangeable, universal kitchen composed of elements to be found everywhere on the planet, just as "grandmother's home cooking" is distinct from international fast food.

prior to eating it. People today contemplate the harmony of colors on walls and on the plate, using the meal as an excuse to discuss gastronomic experiences. In a way, they are re-creating typical market conversations, now expressed as ethno-touristic discoveries. Seated at the table, thanks to the power of the imagination, they conjure up in words—and, it is to be hoped, on the plate—the seductiveness and sensuality of gastronomy, like an evocation of paradise that will awaken the senses in that very hearth of pleasure, the kitchen.

Once the scene of sweaty labor, later the efficient heart of a rational household, kitchens no longer conform to a norm. People can arrange their kitchen as they like, according to personal needs and desires. Rather than imitating some model, the important thing is to find what is essential to you, whether a practical kitchen for enjoyable family meals (*above*, in Provence) or a cool setting for a hot climate (*right*, a pistachio green kitchen in Punta del Este, Uruguay). That is the joy of kitchens today.

château kitchens

Visiting a fine old kitchen means rediscovering the essence of ancient lifestyles. Many French châteaux have lovingly preserved their kitchens, which now offer a delightful trip back in time. This selective tour of France, from north to south, could be extended to include the glamorous châteaux in Versailles and the Loire Valley.

5

To the northwest of Paris, the kitchen of the elegant **château of Boury** (built in 1685 to a design by Mansart) boasts an amazing eighteenth-century fireplace with three hearths. In addition, alongside its fine earthenware and copper objects, the kitchen has a very fine collection of items in wrought iron. Also in the greater Paris region, the lavish **château of Vaux-le-Vicomte** was built in the seventeenth century by architect Louis Le Vau for financier Nicolas Fouquet, and is full of riches including vast underground kitchens lit by high windows. Wine cellars, kitchens, and bedrooms for the "officers" who supervised the service have been magnificently restored with their complete equipment, revealing the nature of a princely kitchen in those days. This is where the famous chef Vatel worked (Vatel later joined the Condé household, where he committed suicide rather than bear the humiliation of being unable to serve the fish course when the seafood delivery failed to arrive in time).

In Normandy, the graceful **château of Vendeuvre** has been inhabited by the Vendeuvre family since it was built in the eighteenth century. It includes handsome gardens, a surprising museum of miniature furniture (with tiny kitchen) and superb underground kitchens that have retained their original furnishings.

In Brittany, several châteaux still possess beautiful kitchens. The **château of Quintin** has a very elegant kitchen all of stone; the few furnishings and objects (a large table, some copper utensils) underscore the splendor of the late-eighteenth-century stove set in front of the large windows. At Concarneau, the amazing **château of Keriolet**, a medieval and neo-Gothic pastiche built in the nineteenth century, possesses a splendid kitchen entirely decorated in fine blue Desvres tiling. The **manor of Plessis-Josso**, in the Vannes region, was built over the centuries and presents the peculiarity of four kitchens from four different periods: a fourteenth-century kitchen with vast fireplace, window seats, and "stew pots"; a sixteenth-century kitchen built in a pavilion next to the original building; a third kitchen outside the residence, at the entrance to the courtyard, which is endowed with a huge fireplace and a bread oven, and was reserved for soldiers and farmers; and a fourth kitchen, from the seventeenth century, featuring the most developed furnishing and utensils (stove, pot hooks, and wooden molds).

The Loire country offers visitors the majesty of France's most classic châteaux, some of which are unjustly obscure. The **château of Lude**, a magnificent Renaissance dwelling, has fifteenth-century kitchens in a large, vaulted underground chamber, in use right up to 1945. Restored in 1993, they are sometimes used for public culinary festivities, such as the traditional preparation of jams and preserves. Two large fireplaces, a bread oven, an extraordinary "piano" endowed with four ovens, a scullery, a dumbwaiter, and an icebox are just a few of the outstanding features on show here. The seventeenth-century **château of La Ferté Saint-Aubin**, built in the heart of Sologne by an Auvergnat with the gastronomic name of Henri de Saint-Nectaire, also has magnificent period kitchens, recently restored on the basis of a 1783 inventory. Everything is in perfect working order today, and a costumed cook prepares delicious dishes from the period while she describes her work to visitors. The nearby refectory sells local produce from Sologne (jams, pastries, wines). In 1939, Jean Renoir chose this charming château for the exterior scenes of his classic film, *La Règle du jeu*. In the Loir-et-Cher region, the **château of Beauregard** is known above all for its magnificent portrait gallery, but its kitchens (in use until recently) are also worth a visit—the superb fireplace decorated with aphorisms, a large table pierced by a structural wood pillar, various period utensils, and above all magnificent copper vessels give life to this fine room of wood and stone. All the great Loire châteaux naturally boast beautiful kitchens that are a delight to visit. Those of **Chenonceau**, large enough to prepare meals for the banquets given by Catherine de' Medici, were set into one of the piers of the bridge over the river Cher, beneath the château. A landing stage was specially built on the river to receive supplies.

 Châteaux and castles provide evocative trips back in kitchen space and time. *Previous page*: The kitchen in Lanhydrock Castle, Cornwall, was rebuilt after a fire in 1881 and has remained unchanged ever since. *Above*: The magnificent vaulted kitchen at the château of Ansouis in Provence, with its copperware, old oven, and impressive stove. *Right*: Two views of the kitchen at the Hospice in Beaune, featuring a vast, double-hearth fireplace dating from the fifteenth century.

Left: The kitchen in the eighteenth-century château of Vendeuvre boasts several treasures, including a fine old stove (along the wall), a collection of copperware, some rare sixteenth-century pottery (on the table), and an ancient coffee grinder (fixed to the edge of the table). *Below*: The kitchen at Quinta de Cardiga in Portugal, once a monastery belonging to the Knights Templar, has one of the largest collections of copperware in the country. *Bottom*: The magnificent Renaissance kitchen at the château of Le Lude, central France, which visitors particularly appreciate in the period of fruit jams and preserves (see the "Connoisseur's Guide").

In the Cher region, the old seventeenth-century bakery in the **château of Jussy** was transformed into a kitchen in the nineteenth. This wonderful vaulted room, with floor paved in fine Charly stone, was used until 1920. It still retains its large oven with spit, its shallow sink, its kneading trough, and above all its kitchen stove.

In Burgundy, the **château of La Roche Pot**, built in the Middle Ages but restored by its nineteenth-century owner, the son of French president Sadi Carnot, boasts a superb kitchen in plain stone with a large fireplace, an impressive multi-stove "piano" range (in the middle of the room, endowed with a system for extracting the smoke via the floor) and a collection of copperware.

Further south, in Perigord, the **château of Les Bories** is a Renaissance dwelling with an exceptional Gothic kitchen complete with ribbed vaulting supported by a central pillar. It features a monumental fireplace with large chimney hooks and bread oven. Worth noting is a spit with a system of counterweights, recently refurbished. A second fireplace stands opposite. The room has remarkable eighteenth-century furnishings, including a saltbox, a tiled stove, a cupboard for copperware, a clock, and a superb central table of wood.

In the magnificent landscape south of the Lubéron hills in Provence rises the majestic sixteenth-century façade of the residence of the Sabran-Pontevès family, the **château of Ansouis**. Among other treasures, it contains a vaulted kitchen dating back to the original medieval fortress. The kitchen features a vast stone fireplace, a collection of copperware, a massive oven from the turn of the century, and very fine old furniture. Finally, in the heart of Provence is another medieval fortress, the **château of La Barben**, which has been continuously inhabited since the eleventh century. Its fourteenth-century kitchen is a marvel—all in fine Provençal stone, under a sloping ceiling, it is endowed with a large fireplace and bread oven, plus a collection of old kitchen items such as spits and jacks, copper vessels, meat tenderizers, bread baskets, flour boxes, kneading trough, and more.

177

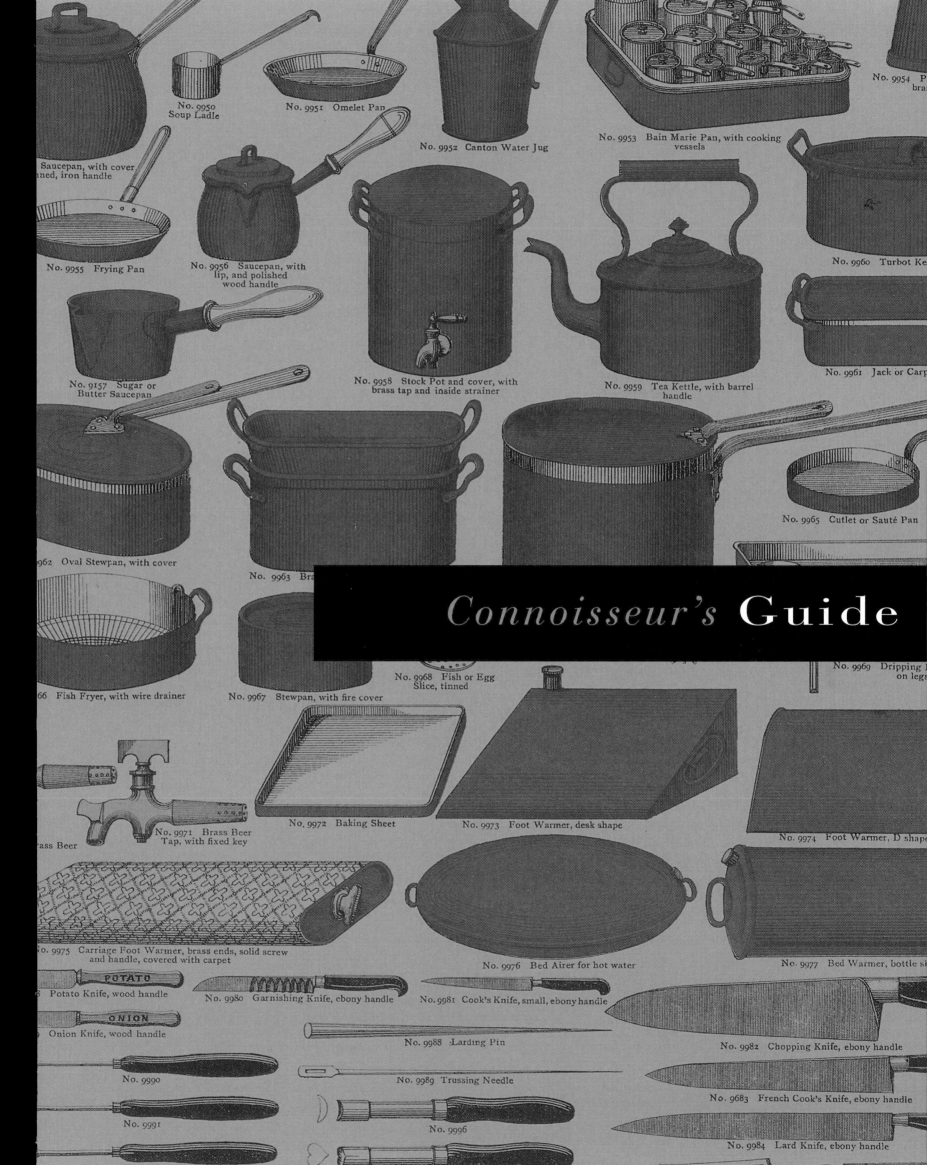

No. 9950 Soup Ladle

No. 9951 Omelet Pan

No. 9952 Canton Water Jug

No. 9953 Bain Marie Pan, with cooking vessels

No. 9954 P_ bra_

Saucepan, with cover, _nned, iron handle

No. 9955 Frying Pan

No. 9956 Saucepan, with lip, and polished wood handle

No. 9957 Sugar or Butter Saucepan

No. 9958 Stock Pot and cover, with brass tap and inside strainer

No. 9959 Tea Kettle, with barrel handle

No. 9960 Turbot Ke_

No. 9961 Jack or Carp_

_962 Oval Stewpan, with cover

No. 9963 Bra_

No. 9965 Cutlet or Sauté Pan

_66 Fish Fryer, with wire drainer

No. 9967 Stewpan, with fire cover

No. 9968 Fish or Egg Slice, tinned

Connoisseur's Guide

No. 9969 Dripping on legs

_rass Beer

No. 9971 Brass Beer Tap, with fixed key

No. 9972 Baking Sheet

No. 9973 Foot Warmer, desk shape

No. 9974 Foot Warmer, D shape_

_o. 9975 Carriage Foot Warmer, brass ends, solid screw and handle, covered with carpet

No. 9976 Bed Airer for hot water

No. 9977 Bed Warmer, bottle s_

_ Potato Knife, wood handle

No. 9980 Garnishing Knife, ebony handle

No. 9981 Cook's Knife, small, ebony handle

No. 9982 Chopping Knife, ebony handle

_ Onion Knife, wood handle

No. 9988 Larding Pin

No. 9990

No. 9989 Trussing Needle

No. 9683 French Cook's Knife, ebony handle

No. 9991

No. 9996

No. 9984 Lard Knife, ebony handle

CONNOISSEUR'S GUIDE

The kitchen has always played a key role in daily life, nourishing passions, creating trades, and giving life to new objects. In this section we have selected a number of useful addresses which should satisfy the most demanding kitchen enthusiasts, be they cooks, collectors or simply those interested in history.

RANGES

A handful of kitchen range manufacturers have acquired a reputation for unsurpassable quality. Their products, frequently hand-made, are a far cry from most mass-produced designs, and are often found in the homes of professional chefs and demanding cordon bleu cooks.

AGA

U.S.: AGA Cookers Inc., 6400 Highlands Parkway, Suite F, Smyrna, GA 30082
Tel.: (800) 633-9200
www.aga-cookers.com
U.K.: Aga-Rayburn, Glynwed Consumer & Building, PO Box 30, Ketley, Telford, Shropshire, TF1 4DD
Tel.: (01952) 642000
www.aga-rayburn.co.uk
Invented in 1922 by the Swede Gustaf Dalen and made in England, the AGA kitchen range has a unique design. A single heat source (natural gas, propane, or solid fuel), situated at the base of the enameled cast-iron structure, maintains the two or four ovens and the two hot plates permanently at their respective temperatures. There are two hand-made models (available in several colors), one with two ovens (one steam and one roasting and baking oven), the other with four (steam, separate roasting and baking ovens, plate warmer). The two hot plates—one for quick frying over a fierce heat, the other for stewing—always remain hot thanks to insulating covers. This system, which is both simple (no dials or knobs to turn) and efficient, has been adopted by many cordon bleu cooks, celebrities such as Mel Gibson, Julia Roberts, and Andie MacDowell, and the cooks stationed at the English scientific base in the Antarctic. AGA regularly invites AGA cookbook authors to demonstrate and teach future users how to make best use of the range.

GAGGENAU

U.S.: Gaggenau USA Corporation, 425 University Avenue, Norwood, MA 02062
Tel.: (617) 255-1766
www.gaggenau.com
U.K.: BSH Home Appliances Ltd, Grand Union House, Old Wolverton Road, Old Wolverton, Milton Keynes, MK12 52R
Tel.: (1908) 328360
www.gaggenau.co.uk
The history of Gaggenau can be traced back to the establishment of an iron works in 1681 by Margrave Ludwig Wilhelm von Baden. The company's appliances are characterized by high-quality materials, scrupulous attention to detail and finish, and the sober elegance of their functional forms. In Europe, the United States, and the Far East, Gaggenau kitchens are synonymous with the latest technology. The Gaggenau range includes gas, electric, and glass-ceramic stove-tops, canopy extractors, built-in ovens and microwave ovens, as well as original elements enabling different types of cooking, notably electric grills with lava stones, steam cookers, electric fryers, and sumptuous freezer-refrigerator cupboards.

GODIN

U.S.: no U.S. distributor yet
U.K.: Lawton Imports Ltd, Unit 6a, Bruce Grove, Shotgate Industrial Estate, Wickford, Essex, SS11 8QN
Tel.: (1268) 769444
www.godin-cookers.co.uk
Godin has become a part of the French national heritage. Since 1840, the name

---

---

has been synonymous with good heating. Less widely known are the firm's kitchen ranges, whose quality is every bit as high as that of its legendary heating stoves. The modular Grande Châtelaine, the Palace with two ovens and eight gas rings, the Châtelaine Pro with two ovens and five gas rings, and the Petite Châtelaine for apartments all demonstrate extraordinary know-how. They are made of cast iron with brass finishings, come in numerous colors and with many options, and combine traditional hand-made workmanship with the latest improvements such as self-cleaning ovens. Options include ingenious pieces of equipment such as a projecting counter, an integrated chip pan, and a hot plate for grilling and simmering. Godin's ranges are both reliable and long-lived.

LACANCHE

U.S.: Professional Home Kitchens, 1504 154th Place SE, Bellevue, WA 98007
Tel.: (425) 641-7224 or (800) 570 CHEF (2433)
www.lacanche.com
U.K.: Fourneaux de France, Poole, Dorset
Tel.: (1202) 733011
Lacanche is a small town in the heart of the Burgundy region. The Lacanche kitchen range factory, located in an old foundry dating back to the eighteenth century, perpetuates the tradition of the master founders who used to make stoves for both heating and cooking. The Lacanche company was given a new lease of life about fifteen years ago by a subsidiary of the Valeo group specialized in professional kitchens. The brand has only been on sale to the general public since 1992. By creating a line for domestic use, Lacanche offers an expertise previously available only to professionals. The models, entirely manufactured in France, are enameled in traditional fashion. The kitchen ranges are available in a variety of styles, classical and modern, in a range of nine modular models. Thanks to techniques and materials tried and tested by the greatest chefs, skilled gourmets can now own a range commensurate with their culinary abilities.

LA CORNUE

U.S.: Purcell-Murray Company Inc., Park Lane 113, Brisbane, CA 94005
Tel.: (800) 892-4040
www.lacornue.com

U.K.: Rick Baker Furniture,
13 Palace Road, London, N8 75A
Tel.: (020) 8340 2020
Europe: www.la-cornue.fr
The Dupuy family has been manufacturing kitchen equipment since 1908. Their ranges, said to be indestructible, are built to order and are hand-made by a single artisan using the finest materials (cast iron, steel, solid brass, nickel, enamel). Options include one or two vaulted ovens (a patented design), a solid cast-iron hot plates for simmering, a stone grill, and brass gas burners. The "ready to install" line offers eight thousand possible combinations of options and finishes, from the Petit Château for small urban kitchens to the Château 147 for large homes and big families. La Cornue is also famous for its made-to-measure service: ranges can be designed to the smallest detail for the individual customer, according to his or her needs. But whatever the model, La Cornue are instantly recognizable thanks to their old-fashioned appearance and beautiful traditional brass fittings.

SMEG

U.S.: no U.S. distributor
U.K.: SMEG (UK) Ltd,
87a Milton Park, Abingdon,
Oxon OX14 4RY
Tel.: (08708) 437373
www.smeguk.com
Founded in 1948, this Italian stove manufacturer was a leading manufacturer of kitchen ranges and other kitchen appliances in Italy before expanding in the rest of Europe. From the very beginning, SMEG (Smalteria Metallurgica Emiliana Guastalla) has attached great importance to technological innovation, in addition to high-quality materials and assembly. In 1956, SMEG had already introduced a range equipped with an automatic timer. Today, the company's stoves include electrical timing devices, multifunction ovens, and triple-flame burners for rapid cooking. Another priority for SMEG is design. The company has commissioned several top designers to work on its products, notably Renzo Piano, who created some elegant ranges and ovens in stainless steel. Equally distinctive are the company's refrigerators—true cult objects that can be found in the kitchens of a number of stars. The most popular models have a marked 1950s flavor.

KITCHENS

Kitchens designed by specialist manufacturers provide the ultimate in modernity and efficiency. They enable you to create a room that is pleasant to live and work in. As it would be impossible to list all the quality kitchen manufacturers, we have restricted ourselves to those which are mentioned in the text.

BULTHAUP

U.S.: Bulthaup USA, 153 S. Robertson Boulevard, Los Angeles, CA 90048
Tel.: (310) 288-3875
www.bulthaup.usa.com
U.K.: The Kitchen People Ltd.,
37 Wigmore Street, London, W1H 9LD
Tel.: (020) 7495 3663
Europe: www.bulthaup.com
Created in 1949 by the German Martin Bulthaup, this company shows how to make your kitchen the center of domestic life. Bulthaup has won many prizes and is now a leading manufacturer of designer kitchens, blending the practical with the aesthetic, contemporary design with technological innovation. Ergonomics are a primary concern, with particular attention paid to different working positions in the kitchen. A central element of solid wood, based on the old butcher's chopping block, takes center stage and is a basic component of Bulthaup designs. In 1992, the company launched its innovatory modular 25 system, permitting great flexibility in the organization of space. In 1997, a new modular system, the 20, was introduced, making it possible to assemble a kitchen gradually, element by element, according to the space available, and in a great variety of styles.

MIELE

U.S.: Miele Inc., 9 Independence Way, Princeton, NJ 08540
Tel.: (800) 843-7231
www.mieleusa.com
U.K.: Miele Company Ltd, Fairacres, Marcham, Abingdon, Oxon OX14 ITW
Tel.: (1235) 554455
Europe: www.miele.com
The slogan of this German firm is "always the best." It was founded in 1901 and initially manufactured washing machines. Since the 1970s, Miele has extended its activities to cover fully equipped kitchens in various styles: high tech, "romantic" all-wood, or old-fashioned traditional. All are made with high-quality materials and feature ingenious details.

ROCHE-BOBOIS

U.S.: 200 Madison Avenue, New York, NY 10016
Tel.: (212) 725-5513
www.roche-bobois.com
U.K.: 421–425 Finchley Road, Hampstead, London, NW3 6HJ
Tel.: (020) 7431 1411
Roche-Bobois has just launched Standing, designed by Lino Codato, a new kitchen line which is both elegant and modern. The elements have been designed along the lines of living room furniture, with cherry-wood modules of varying widths and heights which can be arranged according to the space available.

SIEMATIC

U.S.: SieMatic, Two Greenwood Square, Suite 450, 3331 Street Road, Bensalem, PA 19020
Tel.: (215) 244-6800
www.siematic.com
This family business of German origin was founded in 1929. In 1960, SieMatic launched the first "fitted" kitchen, a revolutionary concept of lining kitchen walls with perfectly fitted matching cabinets. In 1988, the company created the first kitchen "without handles or knobs." Six years later, it developed the 7007 MR kitchen (see p. 120), which is characterized by a pure, sober design and high-quality materials. In 1995, it combined modern technology with the nostalgic retro style, marking the beginning of the successful "cottage years." An innovatory company, SieMatic offers quality design and ease of use.

KITCHENWARE

Looking for a jam strainer, a coffeepot, or a good knife? Listed here are a handful of the many stores offering high-quality kitchenware. A good choice of items can usually also be found in large department stores.

BODUM

U.S.: Bodum Inc., 1860 Renaissance Boulevard, Suite 201, Sturtevant, WI 53177
Tel.: (262) 884-4650 or (800) 23 BODUM
www.bodum.com
U.K.: Bodum UK Ltd, Bourton Industrial Park, Bourton on the Water, Cheltenham, Gloucestershire, GL54 2L2
Tel.: (1451) 810460
This Danish company, founded in 1944, is best known for its glass coffeepots with strainers. In their outlets, you will find numerous versions of these ideal coffeepots, with their beautifully distinctive design. The company's range also includes other kitchen items, including teapots, ladles, and skimmers, as well as pots and pans, wine racks, chopping boards, and elegant storing jars.

HABITAT

No U.S. outlets
U.K.: 208 King's Road, Chelsea, London, SW3 5XP
Tel.: (020) 7255 2545
www.habitat-international.com

In this chain of stores specializing in contemporary furniture for the home, the kitchen section is packed with items both elegant and useful. You will find a range of wine racks, glass or metal jars, small stainless steel utensils, and pretty wooden objects. Habitat also sells classic designs (Magimix toasters, enameled cast-iron Le Creuset pans, Bialetti steam pressure coffeepots), as well as a few rarer items, such as a porcelain service for traditional or microwave ovens which you can clad in rattan covers before bringing to the table, stone cookware (stewing pan or table grill), and a chicken stewer for braising fowl gently in the oven. You will also find a Chinese section featuring woks with all their accessories, baskets for steam cooking and, of course, chopsticks.

IKEA
U.S.: IKEA North America Services LLC, 496 West Germantown Pike, Plymouth Meeting, PA 19462
Tel.: (610) 834-0180
www.ikea-usa.com
U.K.: 255 IKEA Ltd, North Circular Road, London, NW10 OJQ
Tel.: (020) 8233 2300
www.ikea.com
This famous Swedish company specializing in ingenious solutions for the home and low prices is renowned for its kitchen department. Here you will find enameled cast-iron pots and pans, Asian woks, knives of professional quality, classics such as wooden draining racks, and wood-and-steel bottle racks—all at irresistible prices. For young people about to set up home, Ikea offers a box which contains all the basic items required in the kitchen (fifty pieces).

THE CONRAN SHOP
U.S.: 407 East 59th Street, New York, NY 10022
Tel.: (212) 755-9079
U.K.: Michelin House, 81 Fulham Road, London, SW3 6RD
Tel.: (020) 7589 7401
www.conran.co.uk
Sir Terence Conran's shops have well-stocked kitchen departments full of beautiful and practical objects, mostly modern in design. The small stainless steel utensils are particularly attractive: skimmers, potato mashers, butter scoops, and apple corers. In addition to simple but indispensable items such as vegetable mills, mortars, chopping boards, boxes, and jars, the store features an amusing "arachnidan" line of citrus fruit squeezers designed by Philippe Starck. You will also find some great home classics, such as the KitchenAid food processor and the Magimix toaster, a perfect match for the

beautiful espresso machine, complete with pressure gauge and chrome switches, designed by Luca Trazzi. Adventurous cordon bleu cooks will find a large section devoted to Asian cooking (baskets for steaming, woks, chopsticks, etc.). You may even purchase a very fine white chef's hat!

U.S.

BOWERY KITCHEN SUPPLIES
460 West 16th Street, New York, NY 10011
Tel.: (212) 376-4982
www.bowerykitchen.com
This store sells professional kitchen utensils and equipment used by Manhattan restaurants, bakeries, bars, pizzerias, butchers, and delis, at wholesale prices. It also stocks used items at lower prices. The online store is at store.yahoo.com/bowery. Also available here are antique and reproduction kitchenware and utensils.

CHEFS CATALOG
Tel.: (800) 884 CHEF or (800) 338-3232 for orders
www.chefscatalog.com
Tailored for cooking enthusiasts, this website has everything a chef could wish for—appliances, cutlery, furniture, bake- and cookware, and entertaining items, conveniently divided by product and brand. It also includes recipes and sale items.

CHELSEA KITCHENS
Corporate Offices, 50 Hillandale Road, Westport, CT 06880
Tel.: (203) 227-1277
www.coppercookware.com
Chelsea Kitchens manufactures professional-gauge, hand-spun copper cookware, coated in tin and fitted with beautiful brass handles. With high-quality items and reasonable prices, every copper cookware fan is sure to find something here. Chelsea Kitchens also sells copper measuring cups, decorative molds, and tea kettles. The company also offers copper care tips, recipes, and information on how to cook with copper.

CRATE AND BARREL
Tel.: (800) 967-6696
www.crateandbarrel.com
Originally opened in Chicago in 1962, Crate and Barrel offers high-quality and affordable products for the home, such as dinnerware, textiles, appliances, cooking utensils, and seasonal gifts. They also have a wedding registry, mail-order catalogues, and specific furniture outlets. There are eighty Crate and Barrel stores across America.

DEAN AND DELUCA
Tel.: (877) 826-9246 or (316) 838-1255
www.deananddeluca.com
Fine foods, kitchenware, wine, and gifts are Dean and Deluca's specialty. They carry their own line of products in addition to gourmet specialties. On their website you can find recipes, articles, barware, bakeware, flatware, graters, grinders, shavers, and even a virtual butcher's shop.

KITCHEN AND HOME
Tel.: (800) 646-5522
www.kitchenandhome.com
From wrought-iron pot racks to behind-the-sink shelving, from kitchen islands to retro bar stools, this site offers kitchen furniture and accessories galore, in addition to more basic items, such as table linen, serving pieces, cookware, bakeware, and dinnerware.

KITCHEN ETC.
www.kitchenetc.com
The website declares Kitchen Etc. to be the world's largest on-line kitchen, and with its listings of fine and casual dinnerware, gifts, furniture, glassware, gadgets, cutlery, crystal, and electric appliances, among many other items, it is hard not to take their word for it. The company also has retail stores in New England.

LECHTERS
www.lechtersonline.com
With five hundred retail stores nationwide, Lechters offers a good selection of basic home accessories, gifts, tools for the kitchen, gadgets, cookware, tea kettles, candles, and storage items.

MARTHA STEWART
Tel.: (800) 950-7130
www.marthastewart.com
Martha Stewart's website allows you to shop from a dizzying selection of kitchen and home accessories, utensils, and furniture. In addition, it offers craft and decorating tips, as well as page upon page of recipes.

POTTERY BARN
Tel.: (800) 922-5507
www.potterybarn.com
Owned by Williams-Sonoma Inc., the Pottery Barn stocks casual home furnishings that are stylish and affordable. The products are exclusive to the stores and the catalogue.

SUR LA TABLE
Tel.: (1-800) 243-0852
www.surlatable.com
Based primarily in California and the western part of the United States, Sur La Table sells appliances, barware, copperware, knives for every occasion and use,

and unique items such as olive dishes and crab crackers. International brands are stocked, such as Rösle knives, Bodum coffeepots, and Le Creuset cookware. In addition, they also have sale items, special events, a catalogue, and culinary programs.

TAVOLO
75 Rowland Way, Novato,
CA 94945
Tel.: (800) 700-7336 for mail order
www.tavolo.com
Tavolo's website, an exclusive partnership with the Culinary Institute of America, is another site for the demanding cooking enthusiast, with recipes, menus, and chef's tips, alongside brand-name kitchenware, tableware, espresso machines, deck grills, and specialty foods.

WILLIAMS-SONOMA INC.
86th and Madison, 1175 Madison Avenue, New York, NY 10028
Tel.: (212) 289-6832
www.williamssonomainc.com
Founded by Chuck Williams in Sonoma, California, after World War II with the aim of selling quality French cookware, Williams-Sonoma Inc. has become a major upscale retailer of products and services for the home. Cookware, tableware, utensils, linen, kitchen furniture, distinctive foods, cooking ingredients, and a large array of cookbooks make up the selection on offer. There are outlets all over the country, plus a mail-order catalogue. The website includes entertaining tips and recipes.

U.K.

CUCINA DIRECT
Tel.: (020) 7581 8065
www.cucinadirect.co.uk
This mail-order company specializes in kitchen- and tableware.

DIVERTIMENTI
139–141 Fulham Road, South Kensington, London, SW3 6SD
Tel.: (020) 7581 8065
www.divertimenti.co.uk
Divertimenti, which describes itself as the ultimate resource for cooks, is an on-line shop specializing in professional-quality cookware and handmade tableware. There are two London stores (Fulham Road, above, and 45/47 Wigmore Street), which offer, in addition to a huge selection of products, a range of services, including wedding lists, copper pan retinning, and professional knife sharpening.

JOHN LEWIS
278 Oxford Sreet, London, W1A 1EX
Tel.: (020) 7629 7711

RETINNING COPPER COOKWARE

It would be a mistake to keep old copper saucepans simply as attractive decorative items, for tin-coated copper is in fact the ideal material for cookware. The problem is that tin wears out, and as soon as the copper starts to appear at the bottom of the pan, it is time to contact a retinner. Although retinners are scarce, the relatively low cost of the operation makes it well worth doing.

U.S.

Rocky Mountain Retinning Company,
3457 Brighton Boulevard, Denver,
CO 80216
Tel.: (303) 295-0462
www.rockymountainretinnning.com

Oregon Re-tinners Company,
2712 North Mississippi Avenue,
Portland, OR 97227
Tel.: (1-800) 547-7014 or
(1-800) 287-7696
www.re-tinners.com

Re-tinning and Copper Repair Inc.,
525 West 26th Street, New York,
NY 10001
Tel.: (212) 244-7896.
www.retinning.com

U.K.

The specialist kitchenware store Divertimenti offers a retinning service for copper cookware (see "Kitchenware" section). You might also try contacting the manufacturer of your pans.

www.johnlewis.co.uk
This well-known department store sells a good range of fitted kitchens, kitchen furniture, and kitchenware.

ELIZABETH DAVID COOKSHOP
1–12 North Street, Brighton,
East Sussex, BN1 1GJ
Tel.: (1273) 729560
Located in Hannington's department store in Brighton, the Elizabeth David Cookshop offers a full range of quality cookware (including Le Creuset saucepans) and utensils, as well as professional knives (Sabatier).

THE KITCHEN SHOP
17 Barnes High Street, London,
SW13 9LW
Tel.: (020) 8876 3775
This shop specializing in things for the kitchen offers a good range of pots, pans, and casseroles, as well as plates, coffeepots, and bakeware.

LA CUISINIERE TRADING LTD
81–83 Northcote Road, London,
SW11 6PJ
Tel.: (020) 7223 4409
This firm specializes in cook- and tableware, pots and pans, barbecue and picnic items, butcher's blocks and coffeepots. It also offers a range of kitchen gadgets, but no appliances.

FRANCE

France is every cook's Mecca, and no trip to Paris would be complete without a visit to the following three stores, true institutions in the world of cooking where every imaginable utensil for the kitchen can be found.

DEHILLERIN
18 rue Coquillère, 75001 Paris
Tel.: 01 42 36 53 13
This store was founded in 1820 and has been run by the same family for five generations. The decor is austere—there are no gadgets or gimmicks here, no designer fads, just good-quality kitchen items of every shape and size. The two main specialties of the store are copperware and cutlery. The former includes saucepans, pots, frypans, double boilers, covers, and gleaming preserving pans. The selection of knives, specially made for Dehillerin, is impressive and includes models for fish, ham, grapefruits, and salmon. Among the thousands of other items, you will find molds, fresh pasta machines, chopping boards, toasters, porcelain mortars, as well as pastry implements. The experienced sales staff are on hand to offer advice.

MORA
13 rue Montmartre, 75001 Paris
Tel.: 01 45 08 19 24
Mora is famous the world over for its baking and pastry ware. Here you will find a very wide range of cake tins and pie plates, including the Flexipan collection, a surprising number of whisks, as well as a good range of Déglon knives and Mauviel saucepans.

SIMON
36 rue Etienne Marcel and
52 rue Montmartre, 75002 Paris
Tel.: 01 42 33 71 65
These two outlets just across the road from each other perpetuate the tradition of a shop established in 1884 by the current owner's grandfather. Simon supplies catering professionals, but twenty percent of its clientele consists of private individuals. The rue Etienne Marcel store, with its magnificent painted ceiling, carries mainly tableware, although you will also find toasters, Magimix food

processors, the Nespresso coffee machine, the excellent Cona coffeepots, Sabatier knives, and the "Speedy cream" for making a perfect whipped cream. The rue Montmartre store is entirely devoted to kitchenware: cookware by Le Creuset in enameled cast iron or Cristel in stainless steel rubs shoulders with excellent knives (Déglon, Sabatier, Au Nain, Bargoin, Opinel, Zwilling, J. A. Henckels, and the Japanese Global brand). There is also a good range of copperware, including frypans, saucepans, and molds. You will also find the classic food processors made by Magimix and KitchenAid, as well as numerous scales and all the small utensils indispensable for peeling, opening, and cutting.

ANTIQUE DEALERS

U.S.

ANTIQUE STOVE HEAVEN
5414 S. Western Avenue, Los Angeles, CA 90062
Tel.: (323) 298-5581
The name of this store says it all!

ANTIQUE STOVES
410 Fleming Road
Tekonsha, MI 49092
(517) 278-2214
www.antiquestoves.com
This store is an antique stove paradise, with models dating from as early as 1750 to antiques from the 1950s. The owner of the place scours the country for all kinds of stoves, including one-of-a-kind items, and can guarantee their authenticity. Parlor stoves, hard coal stoves, gas stoves, beautifully ornamented wood stoves, and electric stoves are just a few of the kinds sold here. They also restore old stoves. The website features photographs of the stoves, along with honest assessments of their quality.

DECORUM
231 Commercial Street, Portland, ME 04101
Tel.: (800) 288-3346
or (207) 775-3346
This address sells decorative hardware and accessories, as well as antiques, including old stoves and kitchen furnishings. The second floor houses a range of old baths and sinks.

HOWARD KAPLAN ANTIQUES
827 Broadway, New York, NY 10003
Tel.: (212) 674-1000
www.howardkaplanantiques.com
Howard Kaplan sells eighteenth- and nineteenth-century antiques, including English and French dining-room tables, chairs, cabinets, buffets, and sinks.

FAUCETS

Faucets are an essential part of a kitchen, and the German company Hansgrohe is particularly famous for its elegant and sophisticated designs. These include: small, ingeniously designed, extractible sprayheads which cover a wider field of action; sprays that prevent lime deposit; adjustable jets that can be modulated to "soft" or "rain" positions; and faucets that can rotate 360°. The hallmarks of Hansgrohe's products are a distinctive purity of design and good ergonomics. Some of their designs are the work of top designers such as Philippe Starck, creator of a faucet that can be directed and modulated with one finger.

HANSGROHE
U.S.: Hansgrohe Inc., 1490 Bluegrass Lakes Parkway, Alpharetta, GA 30004
Tel.: (770) 360-9880 or (800) 334-0455
www.hansgrohe-usa.com
U.K.: Units D1 + D2, Sandown Park Trading Estate, Royal Mills, Esher, Surrey, KT10 8BL
Tel.: (1372) 465655
www.hansgrohe.com

OLD-FASHIONED FAUCETS

For a traditional kitchen, you may want to choose an original refurbished antique faucet, or a reproduction. Here are a few shops where you may find just the right fixture to suit your kitchen.

U.S.

BATH AND MORE
P.O. Box 444, San Andreas, CA 95249
Tel.: (888) 303-2284 or (209) 754-1797
www.bathandmore.com
This retailer of affordable antiques and bathroom furnishings offers reproduction sink faucets, as well as stainless steel kitchen sinks, cabinets, and other items. They also sell the Kohler and Concinnity faucet collections.

LUXURY HOME PRODUCTS
Address from February 2001: 2611 Concourse Road. Apopka, FL 32703
Tel.: (888) 880-9469
www.galleriacollection.com
A specialist in quality home accessories, including copper and granite farm sinks, together with cabinetry, lighting, pot racks, and vintage or contemporary faucets.

THE PLUMBING WAREHOUSE
994 East 20th Street, Suite B, Chico, CA 95928
www.plumbingwarehouse.com
This Internet company stocks, among others, Hansgrohe, Concinnity, and Blanco faucets, plus sink accessories such as garbage disposals, water filters, and sink stops.

U.K.

CHADDER & CO
Blenheim Studio, Lewes Road, Forest Row, East Sussex, RH18 5EZ
Tel.: (1342) 823243
www.chadder.com
Specialists in hand-made taps reproduced from antique originals. They are made out of solid brass which is then plated in chrome, nickel, or antique gold finishes.

POSH TUBS
High Halden, Ashford, Kent, TN26 3LY
Tel.: (1233) 850155
www.catchpolerye.co.uk
This shop sells items such as butler sinks, double farmhouse sinks, and taps, old and new.

EUROBATH INTERNATIONAL
Eurobath House, Wedmore Road, Cheddar, Somerset BS27 3EB
Tel.: (1934) 744466
www.eurobathinternational.com
This company designs and develops taps used in luxury hotels all over the world. They also sell modern and traditional brassware, vintage accessories, and single-lever faucets for the kitchen.

WINSOR ANTIQUES
113 Main Street South, Woodbury, CT 06798
Tel.: (203) 263-7017
Established in 1982, Winsor Antiques specializes in seventeenth- and eighteenth-century English and French antiques, including Delftware, farm tables, wooden bowls, and dressers. Winsor Antiques is a member of the Woodbury Antique Dealers' Association: www.wad.com.

U.K.

ABBOTT ANTIQUES
109 Kirkdale, London, SE26 4QJ
Tel.: (020) 8699 5729
Abbott Antiques specializes in pewter and kitchenware.

ROBERT YOUNG ANTIQUES
68 Battersea Bridge Road, London, SW11 3AG
Tel.: (020) 7228 7847

ryantiques@aol.com
Genuine and atmospheric period furniture, accessories, and details.

THE DINING ROOM SHOP
62–64 White Hart Lane, Barnes,
London, SW13 0PZ
Tel.: (020) 8878 1020
www.thediningroomshop.com
This shop specializes in eighteenth- and nineteenth-century dining-room furniture and reproductions of French provincial styles. In addition, it sells glassware, china, cutlery and table linen. It also makes furniture to order, especially kitchen tables and chairs.

TOBIAS AND THE ANGEL
68 White Hart Lane, London,
SW13 0PZ
Tel.: (020) 8878 8902
Made to order country-style painted furniture and kitchens are the specialty of this store. It also sells antiques.

HISTORIC KITCHENS

All the following houses have kitchens that are open to the public.

U.S.

BILTMORE
Asheville, N.C.
Tel.: (800) 543-2961
www.biltmore.com
Rivaling the great manor houses of Europe, Biltmore Estate, a 250-room, nineteenth-century mansion, was built to embody the finest in architecture, landscape planning, and interior design. Richard Morris Hunt was the architect and Frederic Law Olmstead the original landscape designer for George Washington Biltmore and his wife, Edith Stuyvesant Dresser Biltmore.

DANA-THOMAS HOUSE
Springfield, Ill.
Tel.: (217) 782-6776
www.dana-thomas.org
One of Frank Lloyd Wright's "Prairie" houses, designed in 1902 for Susan Lawrence Dana, who wanted to be able to entertain on a lavish scale. It contains the largest in situ collection of original decorative glass and furniture designed by Wright.

HARRIET BEECHER STOWE HOUSE
77 Forest Street, Hartford,
CT 06105
Tel.: (860) 522-9258
www.hartnet.org/-stowe
The kitchen in this house was arranged according to the instructions set out in

The American Woman's House by Catherine Beecher.

HENRY FORD MUSEUM
Greenfield Village, 290 Oakwood Boulevard, Dearborn, MI 48121
Tel.: (313) 271-1620
www.hfmgv.org
An astounding collection of Americana that depicts the ever-changing worlds of transportation, manufacturing, home life, entertainment, and technology.

MONTICELLO
Charlottesville, VA 22902
Tel.: (804) 984-9822
www.monticello.org
Illustration p. 53
Thomas Jefferson began to design and build Monticello in 1769, completing it in 1823. It is the only house in the United States on the United Nations' prestigious World Heritage list of sites to be protected at all costs. It contains a number of articles from Jefferson's time, including original furniture from the dining room and tea room. There is also a wine cellar and smokehouse.

NAUMKEAG
Stockbridge, Ma.
Tel.: (413) 298-3239
www.berkshireweb.com/trustees/naumkeag
Designed by Stanford White in 1885, Naumkeag was the home of Joseph Hodges Choate, ambassador to England at the turn of the century. It contains an outstanding collection of Chinese export porcelain, antique furniture, and elegant rugs and tapestries.

OLD MERCHANT'S HOUSE
29 E. 4th Street, New York
Tel.: (212) 777-1089
www.merchantshouse.com
New York City's only fully preserved family home from the nineteenth century is a National Historic Landmark. It was built in 1832 and was occupied by the Tredwell family for almost one hundred years. All the original furnishings, pieces of art, and memorabilia have been left the way they were when the last member of the family died in 1936.

CANTERBURY SHAKER VILLAGE
288 Shaker Road, Canterbury, N.H.
Tel.: (603) 783-9511
www.shakers.org
There are twenty-five original buildings on this National Historic Landmark. You can watch crafts being performed in the Shaker style and discover the customs, inventions, furniture, architecture, and values of this utopian society. The original oven designed by a Shaker sister is on display.

SEWARD HOUSE
Auburn, N.Y.
www.sewardhouse.org
A National Historic Landmark. The architecture of this house, built 1816–17, is a mixture of Federal and Tuscan styles. One of the workmen on the house was a young apprentice named Brigham Young, later founder of Salt Lake City.

STAN HYWET HALL
714 North Portage Path, Akron,
OH 44303
Tel.: (330) 836-5536
www.stanhywet.org
A Tudor-style house, built about 1910 for industrialist Frank Seiberling, founder of the Goodyear Tire and Rubber Company.

U.K.

The houses listed below were restored by the National Trust and they all have kitchens of note. The National Trust can also provide you with a list of castles and manors with a "below stairs" theme.
Tel.: (020) 7222 9251
www.nationaltrust.org.uk

CASTLE DROGO
Drewsleighton, near Exeter, Devon,
EX6 6PB
Tel.: (1647) 433306
Open from April 1 to October 31, every day except Friday (open Good Friday); open in March, Saturdays and Sundays; call ahead for preseason visits.
Granite castle built by Lutyens in the 1920s for self-made millionaire Julius Drewe.

CRAGSIDE
Rothbury, Morpeth, Northumberland,
NE65 7PX
Tel.: (1669) 620333 or 620150
Open from April 1 to October 29, every day except Mondays (open bank holiday Mondays)
Victorian mansion and estate created by the first Lord Armstrong.

ERDDIG
Near Wrexham, Wales
Tel.: (1978) 355314
Open from March 25 to November 1, every day except Thursday and Friday (open Good Friday)
This home contains a wealth of eighteenth- and nineteenth-century furnishings and is surrounded by beautiful eighteenth-century gardens.

HAM HOUSE
Ham, Richmond, Surrey, TW10 7RS
Tel.: (020) 8940 1950
Open from March 31 to October 31, every day except Thursdays and

TABLE LINEN

Fine table linen is an essential accessory to fine food. Most well-known department stores will stock a good range of linen tablecloths, napkins, and tea towels. We have selected a few specialists here, some of which retail via the Internet.

U.S.

ANICHINI
466 North Robertson Boulevard,
Los Angeles, CA 90046
Tel.: (888) 230 53 88 or
(800) 553 5309
www.anichini.com
Luxury Italian linens and textiles, plus decorative accessories and custom-designed furniture. The retail store is in Lebanon, N.H.

JAN DE LUZ
Dolores, Carmel-by-the-Sea, Ca.
Tel.: (877) 622-7621
www.jandeluz.com
Traditional French designs, towel embroidery, and monogrammed linen. Goods can be ordered via the Internet and there is also a made-to-order service.

LINENS 'N THINGS
6 Brighton Road, Clifton, NJ 07015
Tel.: (973) 778-1300
www.lnthings.com
Linens and accessories for the kitchen and bathroom.

MADISON LINENS
1220 Broadway, New York,
NY 10001
Tel.: (212) 244-4380
www.madisonlinens.com
This upscale store sells linens that are hand-embroidered in France, Italy, and on the island of Madeira. Choose from damask and jacquard textiles, cocktail napkins and luncheon sets.

PIERRE DEUX
870 Madison Avenue, New York,
NY 10954
Tel.: (212) 570-9343
www.les-olivades.com
French Provençal fabrics (Les Olivades). Also sells dinnerware and faïence.

THE LINEN HOUSE
www.thelinenhouse.com
Fine Belgian linen retailed on the Internet. The dish towels, napkins, and tablecloths come in a wide variety of patterns and fabrics, both classic and fun.

THE LINEN CLOSET
315 Lee Lane Covington, LA 70433
Tel.: (504) 893-2347 or
(800) 449-2918
www.thelinencloset.com
This linen specialist sells woven damask and pure and blended cottons.

MAISON D'ARCEAUX
Tel.: (877) 475-0087
www.maisondar.com
Traditional French table linen.

U.K.

CARRÉ BLANC UK LTD
186 King's Rd., London, SW3 5XP
Tel.: (020) 7352 0060
Tablecloths, napkins, aprons, oven mitts, potholders, place mats, tea towels and more, including a choice of embroidered items.

THE MONOGRAMMED LINEN SHOP
168 Walton Street, London, SW3 2JL
Tel.: (020) 7589 4033
In addition to tea towels and tablecloths, this store sells hand-painted china. For a coordinated effect, bring your linen to the store and they will paint your china to match. There is also a service for monogramming on cotton, linen, silk, voile, and terry.

LINENS PLUS
65 Church Street, London,
NW8 8EU
Fax.: (020) 7724 7236

THE LINEN MERCHANT
11 Montpelier Street, London,
SW7 1EX
Tel.: (020) 7584 3654
www.thelinenmerchant.com
With great color ranges and the ability to mix and match fabrics, this store aims to be able to cater for every taste. They also carry holiday linen, cocktail items, place mats, napkins, and tea cosies, and provide an embroidery service.

IRISH LINEN COMPANY
35–36 Burlington Arcade, London,
W1V 9AD
Tel.: (020) 7493 8949
www.irish-linen.com
By appointment to Her Majesty the Queen. High-quality double damask tablecloths and luncheon sets, hand-embroidery or appliqués on pure Irish linen.

FRANCE

LE JACQUARD FRANÇAIS
For information and outlets, call
03 29 60 09 04.

IRELAND

IRISH LINEN COMPANY
Kennedy Enterprise Centre,
Blackstaff Road, Belfast, BT11 9DT
Tel.: (028) 9062 8212
www.irishlinenco.com

Fridays. Closed December 25 and 26 and January 1
Ham House is an outstanding Stuart house built in 1610 and enlarged in the 1670s. It has particularly fine eighteenth-century kitchens.

HAMPTON COURT
East Molesey, Surrey
Tel.: (2087) 819500
www.hrp.org.uk
Open all year, except December 24 to 26 and January 1
The building of Hampton Court started in 1236, but it reached its full glory under Henry VIII, when he took possession of the estate in 1528 and commissioned extensive construction work. The sixteenth-century Tudor kitchens are astonishing.

HAREWOOD
Harewood, Leeds, North Yorkshire,
LS17 9LF
Tel.: 113 218 1010
www.harewood.org
Open from April 1 to October 29
The Harewood estate includes a large number of historic buildings, mostly dating from the eighteenth century. The kitchens were created by a patron, Edwin Lascelles, who demanded the highest standards. In the 1840s they were overhauled and the old equipment and fittings were replaced by the most modern versions available at the time. A succession of French chefs oversaw operations in the kitchens—a daunting task. In December 1880, for example, 1,295 dinners had to be provided, with over a ton of meat being cooked. The kitchens were restored in 1996, with the original charcoal stove being exposed and all the copperware being returned to the shelves.

LANHYDROCK
Bodmin, Cornwall, PL3 5AD
Tel.: (1208) 73320
Open from April 1 to October 31, every day except Mondays (open bank holiday Mondays)
A late-nineteenth-century house in a high Victorian style. The cavernous kitchen includes an arrangement of roasting spits, a copper *batterie de cuisine*, and a variety of tools and gadgets. Up to twenty servants at a time could be required to help out with kitchen duties.

PETWORTH HOUSE
Petworth, Sussex, GU28 0AE
Tel.: (1798) 342207
Open from April 1 to November 1, every day except Thursday and Friday (open Good Friday and Fridays during July and August)
The grounds of Petworth House were

designed by Capability Brown, and the art collection in the house includes paintings by Turner and Van Dyck.

ROYAL PAVILION
Pavilion Buildings, Brighton,
East Sussex, BN1 1EE
Tel.: (1273) 290900
Open October to May from 10 A.M. to 5 P.M., June to September 10 A.M. to 6 P.M.
Closed December 25 and 26
Illustration p. 99
The Pavilion was built between 1787 and 1823 for the Prince of Wales, who later became King George IV.

FRANCE

Listed below are the kitchens of châteaux or historic homes in France that are illustrated in the book.

Château D'Ansouis, Ansouis, 84240, tel.: 04 90 09 82 70; Château de la Barben, La Barben, 13330, tel.: 04 90 55 25 41; Hospices de Beaune, Hôtel Dieu, Beaune, 21200, tel.: 03 80 24 45 00; Château de Beauregard, Cellettes, 41120, tel.: 02 54 70 40 05; Château des Bories, Savignac-les-Eglises, 24420, tel.: 05 53 06 00 01; Château de Boury, Boury-en-Vexin, 60240, tel.: 02 32 55 15 10; Château du Champ de Bataille, Le Neubourg, 27110, tel.: 02 32 34 84 34; Château de Chenonceaux, Chenonceaux, 37150, tel.: 02 47 23 90

07; Château de Creil, Creil, 60100, tel.: 03 44 29 51 50; Château de la Ferté-Saint-Aubin, La Ferté-Saint-Aubin, 45240, tel.: 02 38 76 52 72; Château de Fontaine-Française, Fontaine-Française, 21610, tel.: 03 80 75 80 40; Château de Jussy, Jussy-Champagne, 18130, tel.: 02 48 25 00 61; Château de Keriolet, Concarneau, 29000, tel.: 02 98 97 36 50; Château de Lude, Le Lude, 72800, tel.: 02 43 94 60 09; Château de Mongeoffroy, Mazé, 49250, tel.: 02 41 80 60 02; Château de Nohant, Nohant Vic, 36400, tel.: 02 54 31 06 04; Manoir du Plessis-Josso, Theix, 56450, tel.: 02 97 43 16 16; Château de Quintin, Quintin, 22800, tel.: 02 96 74 94 79; Château de la Roche Pot, La Roche Pot, 21340, tel.: 03 80 21 71 37; Château de Rosanbo, Plouaret, 22420, tel.: 02 96 35 18 77; Château de Vandeuvre, Vandeuvre, 14170, tel.: 02 31 40 93 83; Château de Vaux-le-Vicomte, Maincy, 77950, tel.: 01 64 14 41 90.

MUSEUMS

U.K.

SHEPHERD WHEEL
Sheffield Industrial Museums Trust,
Kelham Island Museum, Alma Street,
Sheffield, S3 8RY
www.simt.co.uk
By special appointment only,

tel. 0114 236 7731
An opportunity to see how knives were ground by means of a water wheel on a site that operated from 1500 to the 1930s.

FRANCE

MUSÉE DE L'ART CULINAIRE
3 rue Auguste Escoffier,
06270 Villeneuve Loubet
Tel.: 04 93 20 80 51
This house was the birthplace of the famous chef Escoffier and contains a wealth of documents and artefacts relating to cooking, portraits of famous cooks, and around 13,000 menus.

MUSÉE DES USTENSILES DE CUISINE ANCIENS
25 rue Georges Clémenceau,
85170 Saint Denis la Chevasse
Tel.: 02 51 41 39 01
Open every afternoon except Tuesdays, July and August; every Sunday afternoon and on holidays in September and October and from Easter to the end of June
Opened in 1998, this is the only French museum entirely devoted to the history of kitchen utensils (1850 to 1950). On the ground floor, two rooms house collections of utensils relating to cooking. Upstairs you will find old tools used for chopping, mincing, and grinding, as well as a beautiful collection of pressure cookers (the earliest dating from 1913).

CHRONOLOGY

PREHISTORY
About 730,000 B.C., fire is used for the first time, and soon after human dwellings begin to appear.

NEOLITHIC PERIOD
Man learns to master fire.

MIDDLE AGES
At the beginning of the Middle Ages, the fireplace takes its place in the center of the home.

ABOUT 900
The hearth moves toward the wall and the first stone wall chimneys are built (in Germany and France).
About 1392, *Ménagier de Paris* is published (anon.), giving instructions to young brides on how to use kitchen utensils.
Monastery kitchens are built as annexes to abbeys and this monastic model is gradually taken up by secular society, with the kitchen losing its function as a general purpose room and moving away from the center of dwellings.
This medieval model would last until the seventeenth century. However, one can still find centrally placed chimneys in England at this time.

RENAISSANCE
In his painting *A Visit to the farm*, Pieter Bruegel presents a typical kitchen of the time.
1571
In his *Opera*, the Venetian cook Bartolomeo Scappi describes an ideal kitchen and draws up a list of indispensable kitchen utensils.

17TH CENTURY
About 1600
The emergence of the first stoves in the form of flat cooking surfaces.
In 1624, the French architect Louis Savot sets up a hierarchy of eating places according to social rank: large halls are reserved for princes, the dining rooms for lords, vestibules and bedrooms for commoners, and kitchens for the others. The kitchen is relegated to the outbuildings and its size is in proportion to that of the house.
1681
For a century, the order of the "grand couvert" at Versailles sets the norm for culinary ritual, which is copied throughout Europe. Kitchens are now accorded a special place at the periphery of palaces. The first ice houses appear in the form of underground hollows which are used to store ice during the summer.

18TH CENTURY
About 1720
Tinning of pots and pans.
About 1750
Thanks to the rearrangement of the Trianon (at the Palace of Versailles) and the success of the principles formulated in *La Cuisinière Bourgeoise* by Menon, kitchens return to the "center" of the home.
1770–75
Saucepans, which first appeared in France and Great Britain about 1750, are mass produced.

1784–1833
The French cook Antonin Carême, who ran Talleyrand's kitchens, redesigns certain kitchen utensils.

19TH CENTURY
The nineteenth century marks the arrival of the "closed-fire range."
1806
Martin Roth invents the mobile Bavarian kitchen, the so-called "Emperor's kitchen," for Napoleon I and Maximilian Joseph I, king of Bavaria, to accompany them on their hunting forays.
1820
The first Harel kitchen range appears (either brick or stone), ancestor of the cast-iron stove.
A few years later, the cast-iron range appears.
1822
The kitchens of the Royal Pavilion in Brighton, built for the prince regent, the future George IV, are equipped with an extensive set of copper kitchen utensils and plate covers.
1830
The emergence of cast-iron ranges which completely enclose the fire, heir to the traditional stove.
1837
The kitchens of the Reform Club in London, designed by chef Alexis Soyer, typify the move from an aristocratic to a bourgeois style. The plan of the kitchens is based on the Trianon at Versailles and the rooms are specialized according to specific tasks.
In 1841, Soyer introduces the gas stove, which he judges cleaner and more efficient.
From 1846 onward
Mass-production of cast-iron stoves in France begins (Godin-France).
About 1850
The first mixed-function stoves appear, using either wood or gas.
1865
The mecanical dishwasher is invented (United States)
1869
The American Catherine Beecher publishes a key book in the United States, *The American Woman's Home*, which marks the advent of home economics and in which she presents her ideas on the small kitchen in urban homes.
1870
Kitchens are the first rooms to benefit from the introduction of electricity into the home.
1886
A prototype of Pyrex is launched in Germany. A highly resistant glass able to withstand direct heat, it is used to make ovenware.

1900–20
1905
The first fitted kitchens appear in public housing. Development of furniture specifically designed for the kitchen.
1907
The German Peter Behrens, artistic adviser to the company AEG, designs most of the firm's products (arc lamps, fans, clocks, kettles, and electric teapots). This search for modern comfort in everyday objects prefigures contemporary design.

Bakelite, the first synthetic plastic, is invented in the U.S. by L. H. Baekeland.

1913
Christine Frederick's *New Housekeeping, Efficiency Studies in Home Management* is published, in which she applies Taylor's methods to the organization of culinary practices.

1920S
Period of technical innovation.
1918
First commercial refrigerators in the U.S. (General Motors).
1921
First electric cookers.
1923
First Salon des Arts Ménagers on the Champ de Mars in Paris.
1924
The first refrigerating cupboard, the Polaire, is presented at the Salon des Arts Ménagers in Paris.
1925
The Le Creuset company launches its first pot.
A patent is taken out for freezing.
1926
The American company Delco-Light & Co. launches its first model, the Frigidaire.
1924–26
The "Frankfurt kitchen" is designed by Margarete Schütte-Lihotzki. This attempt at rationalizing kitchen space represents a first step toward the "laboratory kitchen."
Northern European countries adopt this model for their public housing.
1927
The first pressure cooker ("La marmite à pression").
1928
The first commercial frozen foods.
1930
Gas cookers become widespread.

THE 1930S AND 1940S
1930s
Unbreakable glass is invented in France under the name Duralex.
1934
Built-in cooker by Frank Lloyd Wright (United States).
1938
An American engineer from the Du Pont de Nemours company discovers polytetrafluorethylene (PTFE), a nonstick material which is a precursor of Teflon.

1941
Use of Formica plastic (patented in 1911) for kitchen furniture (United States).
1945
The microwave oven is invented by Percy L. Spencer (United States).
The first self-service stores selling frozen foods are opened in the United States.

THE 1950S
Period of innovation in the realm of mixers and utensils.
1953
Launch of the Super Cocotte-Minute by the firm SEB, which is refused entry the following year in the Salon des Arts Ménagers in Paris.
French engineer Marc Grégoire, after discovering a way of applying PTFE (nonstick plastic) to aluminum, introduces the first non-stick frying pan, dubbed "Téfal."
About 1955
The first separate freezer compartments appear.
1956
The Moulinex company is founded by Jean Mantelet and the first food mills are sold in France.
The first all-plastic kitchen (United States).
1957
Launch of the Braun food processor (Germany), whose functionalist design was the work of the Ulm school. This concept of "pure form," commonplace today, became an international stereotype.
Steel replaces iron and tin for utensils.
1958
Le Creuset launches La Coquelle, designed by American designer Raymond Loewy.

THE 1960S
1963
Pierre Verdun invents the principle of the blender (fast rotation of a knife at the bottom of a cylindrical basin).
Mobile kitchen by Joe Colombo (United States).
1967
The microwave oven is marketed.
1968
Ceramic first used for stove-tops in the United States.

THE 1970S
1972
Development of the ceramic hotplate by Scholtès (France).
Launch of the Mama pot, designed by Enzo Mari for Le Creuset.
The first built-in refrigerators.
The so-called "American kitchen" (kitchen opening onto the living room) becomes fashionable.

THE 1980S
The "Robot-Coupe" is marketed by Verdun in the United States and Great Britain.
Modernization of home cooking: thanks to the mecanization of chopping, it is now possible to prepare dishes until then restricted to high-class restaurants.
Domestic appliances are taken up by top designers. Architects Michael Graves, Richard Meier, and Aldo Rossi sign a line of homeware for Alessi (Italy).

THE 1990S
The key words are comfort and efficiency. The kitchen increasingly becomes a room to live in and sometimes even includes an office area.
1999
Presentation of the Screenfridge prototype at Domotechnica. In addition to the traditional functions of a refrigerator-freezer, Screenfridge includes a computerized function using the very latest technology: a detailed list of the contents of the fridge appears on the screen. A shopping list is automatically drawn up and transmitted via the Internet to the supermarket. The computer also gives recipes and indications as to the freshness of food inside.

BIBLIOGRAPHY

Brears, Peter. *The Gentlewoman's kitchen*. Wakefield: Wakefield Historical Publishers, 1984.

———. *All the King's Cooks*. London: Souvenir Press Ltd., 1999.

Conran, Terence. *Terence Conran's Kitchen Book*. London: Conran Octopus, 1997.

Davidson, Alan, ed. *The Cook's Room, A Celebration of the Art of the Home*. London: Harper Collins Publishers, 1991.

Diderot, Denis. *A Diderot Pictorial Encyclopaedia of Trades and Industry: Manufacturing and the Technical Arts in Plates Selected from the 'Encyclopédie'*. Edited by Charles-Coulston Gillespie. Mineola, N.Y.: Dover Publications, 1993.

Du Pontavice, Gilles and Bleuzen. *La cuisine des châteaux de la Loire*. Rennes: Ouest-France, 1998.

Forty, Adrian, *Objects of Desire, Design and Society Since 1750*. London: Thames and Hudson, 1995.

Franklin, Linda Cambell. *300 Years of Kitchen Collectibles*. 4th ed. Iola, Wisonsin: Krause, 1997.

Girouard, Mark. *Life in the English Country House*. London: Penguin Books, 1980.

Goody, Jack. *Cooking, Cuisine and Class*. Cambridge: Cambridge University Press, 1982.

Grey, Johnny. *The Art of Kitchen Design*. London: Cassell, 1994.

Hardyment, Christina. *Behind the Scenes, Domestic Arrangements in Historic Houses*. London: The National Trust, 1997.

Innes, Jocasta. *Country Kitchens*. London: Mitchell Beazley, 1991.

Ketcham-Wheaton, Barbara. *Savoring the Past: the French Kitchen and Table from 1300 to 1789*. New York: Scribner, 1996.

McAlester, Virginia and Lee. *Great American Houses and their Architectural Styles*. New York: Abbeville Press, 1994.

Miller, Judith. *Period Kitchens, a Practical Guide to Period-Style Decorating*. London: Reed International Books Ltd., 1995.

Myerson, Jeremy, and Sylvia Katz. *Kitchenware*. London: Conran Octopus Ltd., 1990.

Paston-Williams, Sara. *The Art of Dining, a History of Cooking and Eating*. London: The National Trust, 1993.

Sambrook, Pamela A., and Peter Brears, eds. *The Country House Kitchen 1650–1900*. London: Sutton/National Trust, 1997.

Wesker, Arnold. *Wesker Plays*. London: Penguin Books, 1990.

PHOTO CREDITS

INDEX

ACKNOWLEDGEMENTS

The publisher would especially like to thank Alain Blottière for his precious help in producing this book, as well as all the chefs who kindly responded to our study (see pages 137–44): Jacques Chibois, Ken Hom, Emile Jung, Bernard Loiseau, Jean-Michel Lorain, Marc Meneau, Georges Paineau, Alain Passard, Olivier Roellinger, Michel Troisgros, Roger Vergé, and last but not least Terence Conran and Richard Olney.

The publisher would also like to thank the photographers who gave permission to use their photographs, especially Simon Upton, Johnny Grey, and Claude Herlédan (photographs published with the kind permission of Ouest-France, publishers of a fine series of books on château kitchens). Thanks also to Christian Sarramon and Inès Sarramon for their efficient and happy collaboration on the picture research for this book, Jérôme Darblay, Marc Walter for the photographs of the châteaux of Menou and Champ de Bataille reproduced with the kind permission of Jacques Garcia, Guy Bouchet, Yves Duronsoy, Jean-François Jaussaud, Yves Robic, and Jean Mascolo, who allowed us to reproduce the photograph of Marguerite Duras's kitchen taken from *La Cuisine de Marguerite* published by Benoît Jacob, as well as Margaret Willes and Ed Gibbons of the National Trust, England, the Felix Vallotton Foundation, and the Musée de l'Œuvre Notre-Dame.

Thanks also go to all those who helped produce this book: José Alvarez, Daniel Rozenstroch, Catherine Sterling, Patricia Zizza, Sophie Knoll, head of production at M6 television channel and the programme *Pourquoi ça marche*, as well as Catherine Lavigne, Axel Buret, Pierre Ferbos, Hortense de Tournemire, Anne-Sophie Poudens and Stephanie Carballo.

This book is dedicated to the memory of Richard Olney, author of many books on cookery and wine (Château d'Yquem and Romanée Conti), and whose kitchen, perched on the hills of Sollies-Toucas, was famous among gourmets in France and the United States.

KITCHENS AND KITCHEN EQUIPMENT ILLUSTRATIONS

The publisher's warm thanks go to the following firms for their kind permission to reproduce photos of their products or use pictures from their archives, in particular AGA, Alain Boisserenc (l'Antiquaire du Fourneau), Bulthaup, Electrolux, Gaggenau, Godin, Interior Architecture (Johnny Grey), Lacanche, La Cornue, Miele, Molteni, Norma, Roche-Bobois, Seb, SieMatic, SMEG, and Zanussi.

Grateful acknowledgements are also extended to firms that have been willing to lend us material for taking photographs: the Dehillerin and Simon establishments, both in the Halles quarter of Paris, Cristel and Cuisinox for their stainless steel items, Mauviel for their stainless steel and copper cookware, Cristal d'Arques for their glass cookware, and Culinarion and Le Creuset for their cast-iron ware (see pages 46, 76, 77, 78, 80, 81 and 85).

Finally, thanks go to the boutiques and private individuals who have kindly authorized us to take photographs: Bachelier Antiquités and the owner of the modern kitchen on pages 133 and 138, Christian's for the AGA and Rayburn ranges, and the Goumard Prunier restaurant.